I
will gather
those who grieve
about the appointed feasts,
They came from you, O Zion;
The reproach of exile
is a burden on them
(Zephaniah 3:18).

Contents

The Father's Feasts
(Leviticus Twenty-three)

The LORD, YHVH,[a] the Creator of the Universe, the Holy One of Israel, spoke to Moses, saying,

"Speak to the sons of Israel and say to them, 'YHVH's appointed times which you shall proclaim as holy convocations—My appointed times are these:

'For six days work may be done, but on the seventh day there is a sabbath of complete rest, a holy convocation. You shall not do any work; it is a sabbath to YHVH in all your dwellings.

'These are the appointed times of YHVH, holy convocations which you shall proclaim at the times appointed for them.

'In the first month, on the fourteenth day of the month at twilight is YHVH's Passover.

'Then on the fifteenth day of the same month there is the Feast of Unleavened Bread to YHVH; for seven days you shall eat unleavened bread. On the first day you shall have a holy convocation; you shall not do any laborious work. But for seven days you shall present an offering by fire to YHVH. On the seventh day is a holy convocation; you shall not do any laborious work.'"

Then YHVH spoke to Moses, saying, "Speak to the sons of Israel and say to them, 'When you enter the land which I am going to give to you and reap its harvest, then you shall bring in the sheaf of the first fruits of your harvest to the priest. He shall wave

---

a YHVH: We use these four letters to indicate the Name of the one true God, which is often mistranslated "The Lord." This may be due to the Jewish tradition of not wanting to pronounce His Name, and Christianity simply followed suit. The Father's Name is comprised of four Hebrew letters, יהוה, yod, hey, vav, hey, and there are various opinions as to how it is to be pronounced: Yahweh, Yahveh, Yahvah, Yehovah, etc. Some believe this Divine Name is made up of four vowels, and pronounce it, Ih-Ah-Oo-Ah. We use the four English letters that best duplicate the sound of the four Hebrew letters as pronounced in modern Hebrew (YHVH), and let the reader determine if, and how, to pronounce it.

the sheaf before YHVH for you to be accepted; on the day after the sabbath the priest shall wave it. Now on the day when you wave the sheaf, you shall offer a male lamb one year old without defect for a burnt offering to YHVH. Its grain offering shall then be two-tenths of an ephah of fine flour mixed with oil, an offering by fire to YHVH for a soothing aroma, with its drink offering, a fourth of a hin of wine. Until this same day, until you have brought in the offering of your God, you shall eat neither bread nor roasted grain nor new growth. It is to be a perpetual statute throughout your generations in all your dwelling places.

'You shall also count for yourselves from the day after the sabbath, from the day when you brought in the sheaf of the wave offering; there shall be seven complete sabbaths. You shall count fifty days to the day after the seventh sabbath; then you shall present a new grain offering to YHVH. You shall bring in from your dwelling places two loaves of bread for a wave offering, made of two-tenths of an ephah; they shall be of a fine flour, baked with leaven as first fruits to YHVH. Along with the bread you shall present seven one year old male lambs without defect, and a bull of the herd and two rams; they are to be a burnt offering to YHVH, with their grain offering and their drink offerings, an offering by fire of a soothing aroma to YHVH. You shall also offer one male goat for a sin offering and two male lambs one year old for a sacrifice of peace offerings. The priest shall then wave them with the bread of the first fruits for a wave offering with two lambs before YHVH; they are to be holy to YHVH for the priest. On this same day you shall make a proclamation as well; you are to have a holy convocation. You shall do no laborious work. It is to be a perpetual statute in all your dwelling places throughout your generations. When you reap the harvest of your land, moreover, you shall not reap to the very corners of your field nor gather the gleaning of your harvest; you are to leave them for the needy and the alien. I am YHVH your God.'"

Again YHVH spoke to Moses, saying, "Speak to the sons of Israel, saying, 'In the seventh month on the first of the month you shall have a rest, a reminder by blowing of trumpets, a holy convocation. 'You shall not do any laborious work, but you shall present an offering by fire to YHVH.'"

YHVH spoke to Moses, saying, "On exactly the tenth day of this seventh month is the day of atonement; it shall be a holy convocation for you, and you shall humble your souls and present an offering by fire to YHVH. You shall not do any work on this same day, for it is a day of atonement, to make atonement on your behalf before YHVH your God. If there is any person who will not humble himself on this same day, he shall be cut off from his people. As for any person who does any work on this same day, that person I will destroy from among his people. You shall do no work at all. It is to be a perpetual statute throughout your generations in all your dwelling places. It is to be a sabbath of complete rest to you, and you shall humble your souls; on the ninth of the month at evening, from evening until evening you shall keep your sabbath."

Again YHVH spoke to Moses, saying,"Speak to the sons of Israel, saying, 'On the fifteenth of this seventh month is the Feast of Booths for seven days to YHVH. On the first day is a holy convocation; you shall do no laborious work of any kind. For seven days you shall present an offering by fire to YHVH. On the eighth day you shall have a holy convocation and present an offering by fire to YHVH; it is an assembly. You shall do no laborious work.

'These are the appointed times of YHVH which you shall proclaim as holy convocations, to present offerings by fire to YHVH—burnt offerings and grain offerings, sacrifices and drink offerings, each day's matter on its own day—besides those of the sabbaths of YHVH, and besides your gifts and besides all your votive and freewill offerings, which you give to YHVH.

'On exactly the fifteenth day of the seventh month, when you have gathered in the crops of the land, you shall celebrate the feast of YHVH for seven days, with a rest on the first day and a rest on the eighth day. Now on the first day you shall take for yourselves the foliage of beautiful trees, palm branches and boughs of leafy trees and willows of the brook, and you shall rejoice before YHVH your God for seven days. You shall thus celebrate it as a feast to YHVH for seven days in the year. It shall be a perpetual statute throughout your generations; you shall celebrate it in the seventh month. You shall live in booths for seven days; all the native-born in Israel shall live in booths, so that your generations may know that I had the sons of Israel live in booths when I brought them out from the land of Egypt. I am YHVH your God.'"

So Moses declared to the sons of Israel the appointed times of YHVH (Leviticus 23).

Introduction

A s Believers [b] in the Messiah of Israel, how do we honor Messiah Yeshua (Jesus),[c] and at the same time celebrate the feasts of the Holy One of Israel? Do we simply follow present Jewish traditions, many of which have been developed over the years, or is there something more we need to understand?

To answer these questions we will first address *why* we have the desire to celebrate. Once we understand *why* so many non-Jewish Believers now feel sovereignly called to honor these ancient feasts, our answer will help us reexamine *how* we celebrate. This answer will encourage us, help us understand why we feel as we do, and add a rewarding sense of purpose to our celebrations.

We will especially look at the role of the non-Jew in honoring Israel's feasts, and hope to encourage them to arise and take their part in the Divine plan.

---

b We use *Believer* to describe those purchased by Messiah Yeshua's blood, rather than *Christian,* because the latter title is often misused (Mat 7:23; 1 Cor 6:20; 1 Pet 1:17-19).

c *Yeshua* (ישוע) is the Messiah's given Hebrew name, it means "Salvation" (Mat 1:21). When transliterated into Greek, due to linguistic differences, *Yeshua* became *Iesous* (Ιησους). In Old English, "Iesous" was then rendered "Iesus" (pronounced *Yesus*), and was spelled with a beginning letter "J," which at the time had a "Y" sound. Later the "J" came to have a harder sound, and it came to be pronounced as "Jesus." Since this name is the result of linguistic differences, we prefer to use the Messiah's given Hebrew/Aramaic Name, Yeshua (See "*Is the Name 'Jesus' Pagan?*"by John K. McKee, *Messianic Israel Herald,* Volume 2, Issue 2).

To identify these celebrants, we ask, "*Who are these?*" Could they actually be "of Israel"? Is that why they feel a deep yearning to commemorate her feasts?

As to the probable identity of these non-Jews, our assumption is that the majority (though not necessarily all) are sons of Jacob and are indeed Israelites. Countless Scriptures that validate this truth have been meticulously enumerated in our previous book, *Who Is Israel?* This solution-driven book is causing a worldwide reexamination of the way Believers define "Israel." It clearly shows that the Father is still dealing with "both the houses of Israel" (Isaiah 8:14). We invite you to read this book for a deeper understanding of Israel's divided house—Israel (or Ephraim) and Judah. The book addresses the separate dispersions of the two houses of Israel, and outlines their present call to become a fully reunited house, or "one stick in the Father's hand" (Ezekiel 37:15-28). Additionally, we offer a summary book called *Ephraim and Judah: Israel Revealed*, which provides a concise overview of these teachings.

In our search for the truth about Israel's feasts, we do not propose that Jews become exactly like westernized Christians, or that Christians become exactly like "Rabbinic" Jews. We hope to help raise up a restored Israel that will have some characteristics of both houses, but will walk away from all false religious beliefs and practices and become the nation the Father ordained from the beginning.

The ancient feasts of Israel regularly bring us back to the Almighty. They remind us of His awesome plan for our lives and of His plan for a restored Kingdom of Israel. They also encourage us to rehearse that plan.

The principal gift found in the feasts is that they give us a sweet taste of the Almighty and provide us with times to gather together with His people. He gives us these special seasons so we can come together and learn to fulfill the two great commandments: To love Him with all our hearts, with all our souls, and with all our strength; and to love one another.

However, when it comes to the traditions of the feasts, we must realize that while tradition can be the glue that holds families together, it can also be the glue that keeps people stuck. Therefore, the primary focus of our study will not be on *how* to celebrate the traditions, but on the wondrous answer to *why* we celebrate.

With this book we hope to do what Priscilla and Aquila did, which is to suggest a "more excellent way" (Acts 18:26). It is written to explain more accurately the purposes of our Father's feasts and to suggest ways in which we might help fulfill them in these end times.

It is not our intent to simply create another feast book, for there are countless resource books currently available on this subject. However, most of these books teach about the traditional observances of the feasts, and we will address the feasts from a different perspective.

Our goal is to help you enter into a more deeply passionate and personally rich path of celebration.

We are addressing those who are crying out in their inner being for a more intimate understanding of the Father's present purposes in the earth. We do not want to provide mere knowledge that only leads to further questioning, but instead to present an understanding that touches the profound yearnings of your heart—the part of you that cries out to the God of Israel and begs Him to show you more of Himself.

On a personal basis, my prayer is that this book will help you know how very much the Father loves *you*. I pray that these words will help you catch a vision and know that you are personally part of the Father's end time plan for His chosen people. It is my hope that as you understand about Ephraim and Judah, you will be inspired and filled to overflowing with new hope as you learn anew how to celebrate some very old feasts.

This book is not about the traditions of man, but about the purposes of Israel's God. What we want to present is not about the outward manifestations of celebration, but about deeper spiritual attributes—the very call of God on our lives.

The words on these pages speak of a deep yearning for both the houses of Israel, Judah and Ephraim, Jewish and non-Jewish Believers alike, to enter into more intimate, profound, and meaningful celebrations with the Holy One of Israel. This book is about a desire for Judah and Ephraim to come together and enter into the true spirit of the feasts. It is a prayer in print.

May we together, Judah and Ephraim, learn to celebrate our Father's feasts in all their fullness.
Amen. So be it.

Batya Ruth Wootten
Saint Cloud, FL
November 2001

The Father's Passover Plan

I say to you, I shall never again eat it until...
(Luke 22:16).

We need to fully understand the above conditional clause because final fulfillment of Passover hinges on it. Furthermore, fulfillment of this "until" will require something of us. Seeing the point behind Yeshua's stipulated clause will help us walk through a new door of end time Passover celebration and fulfillment.

Many people gain greater understanding of Yeshua's "Last Supper" (sometimes called "Communion") when they see it presented in light of a *traditional* Jewish Passover *Seder,* or a *Messianic* Jewish Seder, in which traditions are modified and/or interpreted to reflect Messiah Yeshua.[1]

However, if the Father will allow the eyes of our hearts to be enlightened (Ephesians 1:18), we will see a more excellent way that will enable us to move beyond both of these beneficial illustrations.

The traditional Jewish, and later Messianic Jewish, Passover Seders both can speak volumes to Believers in the

---

1 *Seder* means *order of service.* For more information about these traditions, see Addendum A: *Traditional and Messianic Jewish Celebrations.*

Messiah. For example, according to Jewish tradition, before the feast, the mother cleans the home of all leaven.

The night before Passover eve, or *erev Pesach*, the family has a *bedikat chametz*, a search for leaven. They search, because after cleaning the house, the mother places small pieces of leavened bread in key places, and that night the father leads the children in a candlelight search for the leftover *chametz*. When the children find this leaven, the father, feather in hand, brushes the crumbs onto a wooden spoon or paper plate—all of which (feather, container and crumbs) is wrapped up to be burned the next morning.

This family practice can teach us the basic truth that leaven represents sin, and the "temples" in which we live also need cleansing from all sin by the power of the Ruach HaKodesh (the Holy Spirit), represented by the feather.[2]

The traditional Seder includes three pieces of "striped and pierced" *matzah*, or unleavened bread. Unleavened bread is used because our ancestors did not have time to wait for the bread to rise in their sudden departure for the desert. It was called the "bread of affliction" (Deuteronomy 16:3), or *poor man's bread*, because many people believe it was all the Israelites had to eat at the time.

Messianic Judaism teaches that the three matzot speak of Father, Son, and Holy Spirit, that the unleavened bread speaks of sinlessness, and that "striped and pierced" bread depicts Yeshua, Who brought us healing by His stripes when He was wounded for our transgressions (Isaiah 53:5).

Among traditional Jews,[3] different reasons are given for having three matzah. Some teach that two loaves of bread are present on the Sabbath eve table, and a third loaf is added at Passover as a reminder of the joyous nature of this "Festival of Freedom." Some say the three matzah represent the three groups of people found in Jewish religious life: Priests, Levites, and Israelites. Others say there are three because Abraham asked Sarah to make three measures of

---

2 See Exo 12:15,19; 13:7; Luke 12:1; 13:21; 1 Cor 5:6; 1 Pet 2:5.
3 We refer to Jewish people who have not accepted Yeshua as the Messiah.

fine meal for their Heavenly guests (Genesis 18:6).

Though the idea of "striped and pierced" matzah is used to teach about the Messiah, the historical reason for its use has to do with artistic women and the machine age.

Initially, all matzah was handmade, and since it was rolled-out dough, it was naturally circular or oval in form. To keep the dough from rising, perforations were made in it that allowed the air to escape. Ultimately, the women who baked this bread began to make their perforations in very artistic form, drawing pictures in their bread. Since these artworks could take a long time to finish, the rabbis felt they had to step in. To insure that the matzah would not be allowed to rise, and thus not meet the "unleavened" requirement, they decreed that the entire matzah process, from kneading to baking, must be executed within eighteen minutes.

This edict put a real crimp in matzah art. And with progress being what it is, in England, in 1875, a speedy matzah baking machine was invented. So began our era of "striped and pierced" square *matzot*.[4]

Those who appreciated the art form of traditional matzah were not happy with this strange looking square, uniform, uninteresting matzah brought forth by this new-fangled machine.

Perhaps the real reason for the matzah number and form is because the Father chose that representative number and chose to have it "pierced," because He clearly wants to point us to His Son.

The Afikomen

In traditional Jewish Seders, the middle matzah is broken in half, and the second half is called the *afikomen*, which is hidden away until the end of the meal. This Greek word is said to mean, *He shall come again*. Some say it means "that which comes last," because it is like *dessert*, in

---

4 See *The Jewish Book of Why*, Alfred J Kolatch, Middle Village, NY: Jonathan David Publishers, 1981, 1995, "Matzah," p 192.

that it is the last thing tasted at the Seder.

For Messianic Believers, the afikomen can typify our Messiah, Who promised us, *"I will come again"* (John 14:3).

During the traditional meal, four cups of wine are served. Messianic Judaism teaches that in the Upper Room during the Last Supper, Yeshua was following this rabbinic tradition. According to them, it was before drinking the third cup, called the Cup of Redemption, that Yeshua said, "This is the new covenant in My blood" (Luke 22:15-20).

In this manner, the entire Seder celebration overflows with spiritual significance. We will elaborate on these Seder meanings in a later chapter, "Pesach Pictures."

A Messianic Jewish Passover Haggadah

We offer an abbreviated Messianic Jewish Passover Haggadah, which means "the telling of the story" (see Addendum A). This Guide, like the others, may be purchased from Messianic Israel Ministries, or the four pages may be photocopied for personal, home, or congregational use.

The Four Types of Passover

Beyond seeing the many truths in Jewish Seders, we need to see something more. To enter into a more meaningful appreciation of Passover, we first need to see that there are *four* types of Passovers in Scripture. To put this Feast into perspective, we must realize that when YHVH promised the Israelites, "I will *pass over* you," it was not an accomplished fact, but a living promise.

He said He would stand guard over, protect, and defend His children. He would refuse the destroyer entry into their homes. He would cause the destruction to "skip," or "pass," over them. As Yeshua is One with the Father, Passover likewise depicts Yeshua's promise to safeguard those who trust in Him (John 10:30; 14:18; 17:12-26).

To see the four Passovers in Scripture is to see a picture

of the Father's plan of salvation for His children. Our appreciation of this feast is deeply enriched and enhanced as we realize we are in the middle of the Father's present-day plan. When we understand these four types in their on-going, living context, we know that we have yet to experience the most glorious Passover of all. We know that we, Messiah's New Covenant followers, have much to do with the final fulfillment of Passover.

The Family Passover

We begin our year with the season of *Passover*—just as we begin our spiritual lives with *redemption.*

Our Father said of the Hebrew month, *Abib* (which corresponds to March/April on the Gregorian calendar), "This month shall be the beginning of months for you; it is to be the first month of the year to you....for in the month of Abib you came out of Egypt."

He also said, "Observe the month of Abib and celebrate the Passover to YHVH your God, for in the month of Abib YHVH your God brought you out of Egypt by night" (Exodus 12:2; 34:18; Deuteronomy 16:1).

With this first Passover our Father commanded:

"On the tenth of this month let each one take a lamb for themselves, according to their fathers' households, a lamb for each household. If the household is too small for a lamb, then he and his nearest neighbor are to

Picture from the book cover, *Passover Before Messiah & After* by D. & M. Broadhurst. Available through Messianic Israel Ministries.

take one according to the number of persons in them; according to what each man should eat, you are to divide the lamb ...[and] keep it until the fourteenth day of the same month, then...kill it at twilight. Moreover, they shall take some of the blood and put it on the two doorposts and on the lintel of the houses in which they eat it. They shall eat the flesh that same night, roasted with fire, and they shall eat it with unleavened bread and bitter herbs. Do not eat any of it raw or boiled at all with water, but rather roasted with fire...You shall not leave any of it over until morning, whatever is left of it you shall burn with fire. You shall eat it in this manner: with your loins girded, your sandals on your feet and your staff in your hand; and you shall eat it in haste—it is YHVH's Passover. For I will...strike down all the firstborn in the land of Egypt....and the blood shall be a sign for you on the houses where you live; and when I see the blood I will pass over you, no plague will befall you to destroy you when I strike the land of Egypt. This day will be a memorial to you, and you shall celebrate it as a feast to YHVH throughout your generations...as a permanent ordinance"(Exodus 12:3-15).

We are to diligently teach our children about all that the Father commanded us. When they ask, *"What does this rite mean to you?"*we are to answer them with all diligence and patience; we are to be dedicated to their spiritual maturation (Deuteronomy 6:7; 11:19; Exodus 12:26,42; 13:8,14).

The Holy One designated the first Passover to be a time wherein:

♦ Fathers were to diligently teach their children
♦ The family was to sacrifice a lamb for their household
♦ They were to put the blood on their doorposts
♦ The families were to partake of lamb, unleavened bread, and bitter herbs in their respective homes.

The emphasis of the first Passover was on the godly *household*. The Father said it was to be eaten in a single *house* (Exodus 12:46). Thus He established what we will call the "*Family Passover*."

The Congregational Passover

Later, our Father revised His Passover instructions. He moved the location of commemoration from their homes to His Tabernacle. He moved it from *their* house to *His* house. His command to observe Passover remained intact, but He changed the requirements about *where* and *how* it was to be observed.

"Observe the month of Abib and celebrate the Passover to YHVH your God, for in the month of Abib YHVH your God brought you out of Egypt by night. You shall sacrifice the Passover to YHVH your God from the flock and the herd, in the place where YHVH chooses to establish His name....You are not allowed to sacrifice the Passover in any of your towns, but at the place where YHVH your God chooses to establish His name, you shall sacrifice the Passover in the evening at sunset, at the time that you came out of Egypt. Cook and eat it in the place which YHVH your God chooses. In the morning you are to return to your tents. On the seventh day there shall be a solemn assembly to YHVH your God; you shall do no work on it...Be careful to observe these statutes" (Deuteronomy 16:2-12).

At the Temple in Jerusalem, Israelites were to sacrifice their lambs at twilight, and then roast them. This allotted day of sacrifice was immediately followed by a seven-day period called the *Feast of Unleavened Bread:* "Seven days you shall eat unleavened bread, but on the first day you shall remove leaven from your houses; for whoever eats anything leavened from the first day until the seventh day, that person shall be cut off from Israel" (Exodus 12:15-20).

This new, congregational celebration was to take place *in the Father's house.* There, His children would partake of lamb and unleavened bread.

This yearly celebration served as a collective time of commemoration, reflection and remembrance. Thus the Father established what we will call the *"Congregational Passover."*

Choose this Day...

We now must make a choice. All would agree that the above described Congregational Passover instructions were in place when Messiah Yeshua walked the earth. So how did He celebrate Passover in the last year of His life? Did He simply partake of the Congregational Passover as prescribed in Deuteronomy? Was He following Jewish tradition, as defined by the Jewish men of His day, or did Yeshua do something new? Did He change the way in which Passover was thereafter to be commemorated?

When Yeshua offered what is often called "The Last Supper," was He eating of the Passover exactly as outlined in Scripture, or was Yeshua *Himself* the Passover Lamb that year? Did He celebrate that Passover according to the tradition of His day, or did He establish a new tradition?

He could not do both. He had to do one or the other in the year that He was sacrificed for us.

Some people say that at the time of Yeshua there were two Jewish Passover traditions that were commemorated on two consecutive nights. They claim Yeshua offered His Passover meal on the first evening, and then became the Passover lamb on the next evening. But Yeshua spoke strongly against the traditions of men. He said to those who followed *unscriptural* man made precepts, "Rightly did Isaiah prophesy of you hypocrites, as it is written: 'This people honors me with their lips, but their heart is far away from me. But in vain do they worship me, teaching as doctrines the precepts of men.' **Neglecting the commandment of God, you hold to the tradition of men**" (Mark 7:6-8).[5]

Yeshua would *not* have observed Passover according to the traditions of men. He would have honored His Father's instructions to the letter. Therefore, we must choose. Was it more important that Yeshua once more *eat* of a lamb, or to fulfill Scripture and actually *become* the prophesied Lamb?

---

5 Traditions are fine as long as they do not oppose the truth of Scripture.

Paul the apostle declares, "Messiah our Passover has been sacrificed" (1 Corinthians 5:7; 1 Peter 1:19). In that fateful year Yeshua became our Passover Lamb. That year He was offered as a sacrifice at the exact time the Father commanded that the lamb of redemption was to be sacrificed. When the cup of the New Covenant was raised by Messiah Yeshua on that fateful night, *it was the first cup of a new Passover tradition.*

When we see this truth, we begin to understand that new rules were again applied to Passover: Commemoration continued, but the rules were once more changed.

The Personal Passover

Our Father first established the Family Passover and then changed it to a Congregational Passover. With Yeshua, Passover instructions were again modified. This happened when He took bread and wine into His hands and said to His apostles, "I have earnestly desired to eat this Passover with you before I suffer" (Luke 22:15).

Yeshua said He "eagerly desired" (NIV)—He "earnestly and intensely desired" (Amplified)—to eat "this" particular *Pesach* meal with His disciples.

Why was He so earnest in His desire to eat of *this* particular Passover? Certainly He had participated in many Passover celebrations. Why was *this* particular Passover so special to Him?

Because it would prove to be a "Passover" meal unlike any other. The Passover that Yeshua *"desired with desire"* (KJV) to eat would prove to be *different.*

Luke says of the occasion, "When He had taken the cup and given thanks, Yeshua said, 'Take this and share it among yourselves.' ...And when He had taken some bread and given thanks, He broke it, and gave it to them, saying, 'This is My body which is given for you; do this in remembrance of Me, this is the new covenant in My blood'" (Luke 22:15-20).

Yeshua's Passover marked the end of the Old Covenant Passovers and the beginning of His New Covenant Passovers.

While Passover itself continued as a feast, on this particular Passover, Yeshua was sacrificed "once for all," and we have no need for another (Hebrews 7:27). The central focus is no longer the blood of a substitute animal, which only "covered" sin. With Yeshua's sacrifice, the focus became the pure and undefiled Blood of the Son of God, which has the power to remit, meaning to annihilate sin.[6]

Through His death on the tree (cross), Yeshua became our Passover Lamb.

Of this Passover, Paul said: "As often as you eat this bread and drink the cup, you proclaim Yeshua's death until He comes" (1 Corinthians 11:26).

We desire to proclaim Yeshua's death, because in our proclamation we declare that we belong to New Covenant Israel and not to the world.

When we partake of Yeshua's Passover elements, we declare that *He* is our Passover; the angel of the second death will "pass over" us in the final judgement because we are sanctified by the Blood of the New Covenant Passover Lamb. Through Yeshua we have an eternal sacrifice for our sins. Thus we are called the eternal "Israel of God" (Galatians 6:16).[7]

With Yeshua's Passover there came a certain fulfillment of, and another modification in, the Passover ordinance.

In and through Him, the focus of Israel's priesthood was changed from the Aaronic order to that of Melchizedek: "When the priesthood is changed, of necessity there takes place a change of law also." The sacrifices were finished.

Yeshua is our eternal High Priest according to the order of Melchizedek (Hebrews 5:6; 7:12), and as our Eternal High Priest, He instructed us to partake of *different Passover elements*.

---

6 Acts 20:28 speaks of "the church of God which He purchased with His own blood." Therefore, it was "God['s]...blood." See 1 Pet. 1:19; Heb 9:14, also see the book, *Who Is Israel?* chapter 10, "The Blood, The Redeemer and Physical Israel" and the "Addendum."

7 Eph 2:13-14; Col 1:20; Luke 22:16; Rom 5:9; Eph 1:7-14; Heb 9:12,15,26; 13:11-12,20.

In the past, the prescribed elements were lamb and unleavened bread, but in the New Covenant the prescribed elements are bread and wine. Why?

Unlike the old Passover sacrifices, Yeshua's sacrifice is not an annual event, as was the slaying of Passover lambs. Rather, He is our ever-present, ever-available sacrifice. Commemoration of His sacrifice includes the elements from the prescribed *daily offering:* Bread and Wine.[8]

Yeshua also moved the *emphasis* of our search for leaven. Leaven typifies sin, and all leaven was to be removed from their houses for the Feast of Unleavened Bread, which immediately followed Passover. Yeshua moved the *emphasis* of that search to the areas of our hearts. That is why Paul instructs us to "clean out the old leaven of wickedness and malice from your hearts" (Matthew 15:18; 1 Corinthians 5:7).

In addition to having outward symbols of our faith that can help keep us on track, Yeshua wants us to deal with our hearts. "Behold," He says, "I stand at the door [of the heart] and knock....If anyone hears My voice and opens the door, I will come in to him and will sup with him, and he with Me" (Revelation 3:20).

We will call the Passover established by Messiah Yeshua the *Personal Passover*, for only those on whose heart's door He has knocked can invite Him into their lives. Only those who have personally invited Yeshua into their lives are called to partake of His intimate Passover Supper.

If you have not yet done so, invite Yeshua into your life right now. You do not need anyone to lead you in a particular prayer. You simply need to repent of your sins and ask Yeshua to come into your heart and be Lord of your life.

The Kingdom Passover

When Yeshua initiated the New Covenant Passover, He

---

8 See Heb 7:27; 9:12; 10:10; 1 Pet. 3:18; Exo 29:40-42; Num 15:1-13; 28:5-7. Though incorporated into Jewish Seders, partaking of wine at Passover was *not* commanded in Scripture.

lifted high the broken bread and said to His disciples, "I shall never again eat it *until* it is fulfilled in the kingdom of God." When He had taken the cup and given thanks, He said, "Take this and share it among yourselves; for I say to you, I will not drink of the fruit of the vine from now on *until* the kingdom of God comes" (Luke 22:15-18).

In saying this, Yeshua foretold a coming, glorious, eternal Passover, one that will be celebrated in the Kingdom of God. For there is a glorious Passover that is yet to come. It will take place at the Marriage Supper of the Lamb, and blessed are those who are invited to it (Revelation 19:9). One day the trumpet will sound, and we who are invited will put on imperishable wedding garments,[9] for we have been invited to a transcendent celebration.

At that time the believing family of Israel will again be "passed over." As overcomers, the second death will not be able to harm us. In utter jubilation we will ask: "Where O death is your victory? Where O death is your sting?" (Hosea 13:14; 1 Corinthians 15:55; Revelation 21:7).

Messiah Yeshua will again take the cup into His hands as prophesied, and, perhaps in honor of the rabbinic custom of His Jewish brothers, He will call it *the fourth Passover Cup*, which is known as *the Cup of Praise*.

That would certainly be an appropriate title, for when Messiah lifts high *that* cup, Hallelujah's that will ring for an eternity will begin. Death, finally and forevermore, will be swallowed up in victory.[10]

When we celebrate *that* Passover, then we will know the full and eternal glory of the *Kingdom Passover*.

Father, by your grace and mercy may we come to know the joy of that celebration!

---

9 See 1 Cor. 15:51-57; Mat 22:1-14; Hos 13:14; Rev 19:7-9, and the book, *Who Is Israel?* chapter 17, "From Orphans To Heirs."

10 Rev 2:11; 20:6,14; 21:8; Hos 13:14; 1 Cor 15:55.

Celebrating Passover As Never Before!

Passover can depict many things to us. In the Family Passover we see that the Father wants to save our families, for He told us to "take enough lamb for the whole household." Yeshua is the "*Lamb*" [11] and we can trust that there is enough of Him for our whole family—all who have a heart for Him will be satisfied.

As Messiah Yeshua's people, we need to bring our families to the Lamb. A healthy, happy family that is obedient to the Father because of their love for Him is a powerful witness. It is a witness that will encourage others to seek to belong to the God of Israel.

The Father also wants to save us as a congregation, because there are things He can accomplish in our lives only when we are gathered in an assembly with those of like faith. We can experience congregational worship, the Body can minister to one another, and we can be built up in our faith.

Additionally, the Father wants our salvation to be very

---

11 John 1:29; Pet. 1:19; Rev 5:6.

personal so we will learn to hear His voice for ourselves[12] and to have the faith of our forefather Abraham. We are heirs of his promise. Our God promised to provide "Himself" as a Sacrifice and to be a personal God to Abraham's children (Galatians 2:29; Genesis 22:8; 17:7).

Finally, the Father desires to save us as a kingdom. His ultimate goal is for us to be a kingdom of priests and to bring His Kingdom of Israel here to this earth.[13]

Speaking in broad terms, let us say that for a season, YHVH put emphasis on the Family Passover to teach His people the need for godly families. Then He emphasized the Congregational Passover to establish the need for fellowship. Finally, He moved the focus to the Personal Passover so we can learn to hear His voice (John 10:27).

We are now entering into a new day. Once more the Father is moving His emphasis. The God of Israel is doing a new thing: He is making the two sticks of Ephraim and Judah one in His hand. He will soon bring forth an invincible, blameless army comprised of sons who are able to take His Land. When the two houses of Israel unite as brothers they will become a mighty army. Together they serve YHVH Tzevaot, "YHVH of Hosts, the God of the armies of Israel" (Ezekiel 37:15-28; 1 Samuel 17:45). When Ephraim and Judah are fully reunited in Yeshua, when He is reigning in the Promised Land and is the King of kings over the whole house, then we will celebrate the Kingdom Passover.[14]

We who see this Passover plan must work toward its fulfillment. We must proclaim the full, liberating, enlightening truth about Passover. We must work to reunite the two houses of Israel, that we might celebrate the most glorious of all Passovers.

The Passover Plan: It was, it is, and it is to come. It is a precious promise that is alive with new meaning.

---

12 See Eph 4:15; Heb 6:1-3; 1 Tim. 2:5.
13 See Mat 6:10; Act 1:6; 1 Pet. 2:9; Rev 1:6; 5:10; 20:6; 21:2.
14 See Isa 11:13-14; Obad 1:18; Zech 9:13; Amos 9:10; Zeph 3:11-13.

Celebration Suggestions

To celebrate the four Passovers, gather four families, groups, or individuals and assign to each a Passover: *Family, Congregational, Personal, or Kingdom.*

Also assign to each a side of the room in which you choose to meet: north, south, east, or west. When you gather, have the youngest son present ask the famous Passover question:

" *Why is this night different from all other nights?*"

Let each family take turns portraying, explaining, acting out, preaching about, or just rejoicing over, their particular Passover expression. If you do not have enough people available to play the roles, you can make and paint cardboard cutouts of the drawings found in this chapter. The leader can take the group to each venue and then explain each particular Passover. Make your gathering as elaborate or simple as you wish.

For example, you may want to have everyone dress in costume, and at each Passover station offer the guests the prescribed offering for that particular Passover.

Put the *Family Passover* station in front of a doorway and tape paper "blood" to the posts and lintel, then have a

family offer the three prescribed elements: a small piece of roast lamb, unleavened bread, and bitter herbs. Invite them in and encourage all to eat the Passover "quickly."

For the *Congregational Passover*, have someone dress as the High Priest, make an altar and put a sacrificial lamb on it (use a stuffed toy or make one from stuffed socks). Have the changes in the scriptural command (see the Passover Guide) written out

on a scroll (a rolled up paper), and have the priest read it as though it were a declaration being made to ancient Israel.

At this station have everyone partake of the prescribed elements of roast lamb, unleavened bread, and bitter herbs.

For the *Personal Passover*, feature Messiah Yeshua and the apostles reclining at a table. Here, talk about having a clean heart, one that is ready to receive Messiah's sacrifice (Psalm 51:10; 1 Corinthians 11:27-31). Then offer the Believers the New Covenant Passover Bread and Wine: The Body and Blood of our Messiah.

At the *Kingdom Passover* station, display fruits, flowers, and food to represent the endless, bountiful table from which we will partake at the Marriage Supper of the Lamb.

Decorate the table with candlesticks, a menorah, pretty brass and glass items, and so on. Try using a mirror draped in fabric and twinkle lights as a backdrop. Use anything and everything that will make your table look lush and beautiful.

Once each Passover is explained or acted out, let everyone gather in the center of the room to gaze around and appreciate the Father's glorious plan of redemption. First, that we should be raised in godly homes by godly fathers who teach their children the way of righteousness. Second, that godly congregations declare Israel's need for a covering

for sin and aid them in finding that way to righteousness. This is the ideal way for each of us to find the way to the One who gives us the Personal Passover.

In this way our children can more readily find their way to Him, because they will have seen a pattern of righteousness in their fathers, their families, and their congregations.

Explain to everyone that when these standards of righteousness are met in the hearts of our people (Isaiah 27:9; Zephaniah 3:18), when Ephraim and Judah become one stick in the Father's hand (Ezekiel 37:15-28), then we will be ready to join Messiah for the Kingdom Passover—the one that will take place in *B'olam Haba*, the eternal Kingdom to come.

Lamb Recipe
Four Passovers Celebration Guide

On the following pages we offer an excellent roast lamb recipe, in addition to four pages taken from our *Four Passovers Celebration Guide.* Like our other Guides, this too is offered for sale by Messianic Israel Ministries. You can order a printed and folded 5 1/2 x 8 1/2 copy to keep in your Bible, or you may photocopy the four copyrighted pages for use in home or congregational celebrations.

Celebration Guides are offered for sale in the Key of David Publications section of the book.

Roast Lamb Shank
With Herbs

Combine: Half ( ) teaspoon each:
powdered ginger, thyme, sage, marjoram.
One (1) teaspoon each: salt, pepper.
One (1) tablespoon each: soy sauce, olive oil.
One each: clove of crushed garlic, bay leaf.
Make slits in lamb, rub marinade into and on meat.
Marinate for at least one hour or overnight.
Place lamb in uncovered roasting pan, roast at 300° F.
(18 minutes per pound for well done, 12 for rare.)
Recipe may be doubled for stronger flavor.

Come . . .
Let Us Rehearse
The Four Passovers

*"And on the first day you shall have a holy assembly—
a miqra kodesh—a holy rehearsal" (Exodus 12:16).
We assemble because we love the Holy One of Israel—
and His Son, our Redeemer, Yeshua, Messiah of Israel.
We have a miqra because we love our Jewish brothers.
We rehearse because we long for the restoration of
the whole house of Israel . . .*

Angus and Batya Wootten
Messianic Israel Ministries
PO Box 700217, Saint Cloud, FL 34770

Phone 800 829-8777   Web Site: www.mim.net

The Family Passover

Before the first Passover, the Holy One declared: "On the tenth of this month let each one take a lamb for themselves, according to their fathers' households, a lamb for each household....you shall keep it until the fourteenth day of the same month, then...kill it at twilight. Moreover, they shall take some of the blood and put it on the two doorposts and on the lintel of the houses in which they eat it. They shall eat the flesh that same night, roasted with fire, and with unleavened bread and bitter herbs. Do not eat any of it raw or boiled with water, but roasted with fire...You shall... eat it in haste—it is the YHVH's Passover. For I will ...strike down all the firstborn in the land of Egypt....and the blood shall be a sign for you on the houses where you live; and when I see the blood I will pass over you, and no plague will befall you to destroy you when I strike the land of Egypt. Now this day will be a memorial to you, and you shall celebrate it as a feast to YHVH; throughout your generations you are to celebrate it as a permanent ordinance" (Exodus 12:3-15).

As priests of their homes, our forefathers were to teach their children about YHVH's deliverance of His people when their sons asked the question, "What does this rite mean to you?" YHVH designated Passover as a time for *fathers* to diligently teach their children. It also marked a time to sacrifice a lamb for the household, to put the blood on their doorposts, and to have their families partake of lamb, unleavened bread, and bitter herbs in their homes.

The emphasis of this Passover is on the godly "household." For He commanded that it "be eaten in a single house" (Deut 6:7; 11:19; Exodus 12:26,42,46; 13:8,14). Thus He established the "*Family Passover.*"

The Congregational Passover

Later, the Father changed the Passover instructions. He moved the rite from their homes to the Tabernacle—from *their* house to *His* house: "Observe the month of Abib and celebrate the Passover to YHVH your God, for in the month of Abib YHVH your God brought you out of Egypt by night. You shall sacrifice the Passover to YHVH your God from the flock and the herd, in the place where YHVH chooses to establish His name."

For seven days our forefathers ate unleavened bread and remembered the Exodus. Leaven was not to be seen in all their territories. "You are not allowed," commanded YHVH, "to sacrifice the Passover in any of your towns, but at the place where YHVH your God chooses to establish His name, you shall sacrifice the Passover in the evening at sunset, at the time that you came out of Egypt. Cook and eat it in the place which YHVH your God chooses....Be careful to observe these statutes" (Deut 16:2-12; Exodus 12:2).

This "congregational" celebration took place in YHVH's house. There, as the priests led them in a collective time of remembrance, they partook of lamb, bitter herbs, and unleavened bread. Thus did YHVH establish the "*Congregational Passover.*"

©BRW

The Personal Passover

Passover instructions were again changed when Messiah Yeshua took the bread and wine into His hands. He said to His apostles, "I have earnestly desired to eat *this* Passover with you before I suffer." And, "having taken bread and given thanks, He broke it, and gave it to them, saying, 'This is My body which is given for you; do this in remembrance of Me.' And in the same way He took the cup after they had eaten, saying, 'This cup which is poured out for you is the new covenant in My blood'" (Luke 22:15-20; Matt 26:26-29).

Yeshua's Passover marked the last of the Old Covenant Passovers and the first New Covenant Passover. No longer would the central focus be the blood of a substitute animal, which only "covered" sin. Rather, the focus became that of the pure, undefiled Blood of the Son of God that remits, even annihilates sin.

Through His death on the tree, Yeshua became our Passover Lamb. For "Messiah, our Passover, has been sacrificed" (1 Cor 5:7). Of this Passover, Paul explained: "As often as you eat this bread and drink the cup, you proclaim Yeshua's death until He comes."

We proclaim Yeshua's death, because in doing so we declare that we belong to New Covenant Israel and not to the world. We proclaim that He is *our* New covenant Passover Lamb so the angel of the second death will *pass over* us in the final judgement. Because we are sanctified and covered with the Blood of Yeshua, we have an eternal sacrifice for our sins. In Him, we are the eternal Israel of God (1 Cor 11:26; Eph 1:7-14; 2:13-14; Col 1:20; Luke 22:16; Rom 5:9; Heb 9:12,15,26; 13:11-12,20; Gal 6:16).

With Yeshua's Passover came a change in the Passover law. For "when the priesthood is changed, of necessity there is a change of law also" (Heb 5:6; 7:12). Israel's priesthood was changed from the Aaronic order to that of the High Priest, according to the order of Melchizedek—to Yeshua's priesthood. Through Messiah, Israel's Passover law was changed to observance of the New Covenant Passover.

As our High Priest, Yeshua instructed us to partake of His "bread and wine." His is not an annual occurrence like the old sacrifice, but is an ever-present, ever-available sacrifice, and so includes elements from the daily offering: Bread and Wine (Heb 7:27; 9:12; 10:10; 1 Pet 3:18; Exodus 29:40-42; Num 15:1-13; 28:6).

Yeshua "knocks at the door of our heart" because He moved the emphasis of our Passover search for leaven: We are to "clean out the old leaven of wickedness and malice from our hearts" (Rev 3:20; 1 Cor 5:7). He wants us to experience more than mere outward symbols of our faith: He wants us to deal with our hearts, that we might live righteous lives. To help us accomplish this otherwise impossible task, He became our personal Passover Lamb.

Thus did our Messiah establish the "*Personal Passover.*" ©BRW

The Kingdom Passover

When Yeshua initiated the New Covenant Passover, He said He "desired with desire" to partake of "this Passover," for it was to be a Passover unlike any other...

Yeshua also said: "I shall never again eat it until it is fulfilled in the kingdom of God." And when He had taken the cup and given thanks, He said, "Take this and share it among yourselves; for I say to you, I will not drink of the fruit of the vine from now on until the kingdom of God comes" (Luke 22:15-18).

In saying this, Messiah was foretelling a coming, glorious, eternal Passover, one that will be celebrated in "the kingdom of God." There is a Passover yet to come. This celebration is called "the Marriage Supper of the Lamb," and "blessed are those who are invited to it." One day the trumpet will sound and Believers will put on our imperishable wedding garments, for we are invited to a transcendent celebration (1 Cor 15:51-57; Mat 22:1-14; Hos 13:14; Rev 19:7-9).

At that celebration, the believing family of Israel will again be "*passed over*." The second death will not be able to harm us because we are *overcomers*. Then we will ask: "Where O death is your victory? Where O death is your sting?" As promised, Messiah will *again* take the cup into His hands—the Passover Cup of Praise. Then Hallelujah's that will ring for an eternity will begin, for death will be forever swallowed up in victory! (Rev 2:11; 20:6,14; 21:8; Hos 13:14; 1 Cor 15:55).

We who are overcomers must help establish this Kingdom Passover!

We who long to celebrate Passover must have an ever-present desire for this Kingdom Passover in *our* hearts. For we will not, we cannot, celebrate it until the house of Israel is fully reunited. To celebrate *this* Passover, Israel's Kingdom must be restored. And the Father's prescribed plan for the restoration of *all* Israel is to have those of the "wild" side of the family of Israel provoke those of Judah to want what they have.

To bring about this reunion, the other house of Israel, those of Ephraim, those destined to become a "*melo hagoyim*," or "the fullness of Gentiles"—their jealousy of Judah must depart. This will happen when they see the truth of their *own* Israelite roots. It will happen when they begin to walk as one who is neither superior, nor inferior, to Judah, but as one who sees Judah as an Israelite brother. This is YHVH's plan of salvation for *all* Israel (Gen 48:19; 2 Sam 19:43; 1 Kings 11:31; 2 Chr 11:4; Isa 8:14; 11:13; Jer 31:18-19; Hos 1-2; Amos 9:9-11; Matt 12:25; Acts 15:16-17; Rom 8:15-17,23; 9:4; 11; Gal 4:5; Eph 1:5).

When Ephraim sees the truth about all Israel, about his own Israelite roots, and about his call to *rehearse*, then the reunion will begin.

"Let us therefore celebrate the feast..." (1 Cor 5:7).

Dedicating Your Home

Passover is an excellent time to dedicate our homes to the God of Israel. Just as our forefathers painted the blood of the lamb on the doorposts of their homes, we need to envision our entire home being covered by the Blood of Yeshua—the Blood that protects from all evil.

Yeshua is the Door

Yeshua asks us to open the door of our hearts to Him. When we do, He in turn opens a door: It is a door of salvation, one that leads to Heaven's Gate, and to protection from the second death. It is the door of Passover. Beyond this Passover Door lies the Beautiful Land—a land of peace and harmony—the Land of the Israel of God.

Let us respond to Yeshua's call to come and dine at the Father's Table. Come. Gather your family, friends, and loved ones. Come and celebrate the Feast of Passover.

Marking Earthly Doors

You can begin your home dedication by affixing a *mezuzzah* to your doorpost (see instructions below). Then you can have a celebration by offering a meal of roast lamb, unleavened bread, and bitter herbs. With family gathered around, let everyone take time to remember how the Father has personally delivered them from the "bondages of Egypt." Let them rejoice over that deliverance. Finally, after everyone has examined their hearts, let all partake of the Body and Blood of the Lamb.

Remind everyone that Abib, the Passover month, marks the head of the year (Exodus 12:2), so now is the time to make "New Years Resolutions." Now is the time to dedicate ourselves to righteous acts, for they will be our only garments at the coming wedding feast of the Lamb (Matthew 22:11; Revelation 19:8-9).

You Shall Write Them On Your Doorposts... The Mezuzzah

Mezuzzah Scroll: Front and Back

Our Father instructed the sons of Israel to write His commandments on their doorposts and gates. From ancient times our Jewish brothers have followed this custom and have affixed *mezuzzahs* to their doorposts.

Even before Yeshua walked the streets of Jerusalem, before entering the home, it was the custom to touch the mezuzzah and then to touch the fingers to the lips as a reminder that the Word of God was always to be on the lips of His people.

A mezuzzah can serve to identify the homes of God's chosen people just as the blood on the doorposts served to identify them when the angel of death passed over their homes in Egypt.

The Hebrew word *mezuzzah* means *doorpost.* Traditionally, a parchment scroll with Scripture verses written in Hebrew is rolled up and placed in the mezuzzah cover (see above pictures). *Kosher* mezuzzah scrolls are hand written in Hebrew by a Scribe. Compared to the relatively inexpensive, mass-produced parchments used by most, the hand-written scrolls are very expensive.[15]

The traditional mezuzzah cover contains a scroll with Deuteronomy 6:9 and 11:13-21 Scriptures printed on it:

"Hear O Israel! YHVH is our God, YHVH is one! And you shall love YHVH your God with all your heart and with all your soul and with all your might. And these words, which I am commanding you today, shall be on your heart, and you shall teach them repetitively to your children. You must talk about them, when you are sitting at home, when you are on the road, when you are busy, and when you are at rest. And you shall bind them as a sign upon your hand, and let them serve as a symbol on your forehead. And you shall write them on the doorposts of your houses, and on your gates...And it shall come about, if you listen obediently to My commandments which I am commanding you today, to love YHVH your GoD and to serve Him with all your soul, I will give your land rain in season, autumn rain and spring, that you may gather in your grain and your new wine and your oil. And I will give grass in your fields for your cattle, and you shall eat and be satisfied. Beware, lest your hearts be deceived and you turn away and serve other gods and worship them. For YHVH's anger will flare up against you, and He will shut up the Heavens so that there will be no rain and the ground will not yield its fruit; and you will perish quickly from the good land which YHVH is giving you. You shall therefore impress these words of mine on your heart and on your soul; and you shall bind them as a sign on your hand, and they shall be as a symbol on your forehead. And you shall teach them to your children, speaking of them at home and abroad, when you lie down and when you rise up. And you shall post them on the doorposts of your house and on your gates. So that your days and the days of your children may be multiplied in the land which YHVH swore to your fathers to give them, as long as the Heavens remain above the earth."

---

15 Mezuzzot are available at <www.mim.net> and on the Internet.

El Shaddai

שׁ דַּ י׃

*Hebrew letters
sheen, dalet,
yod spell
Shaddai
(read from
right to left)*

Mezuzzot (plural) covers come in many different styles and finishes. Most have the name *Shaddai*, or the initial letter for *Shaddai*, the Hebrew letter, *sheen*, written on the front. The name, *El Shaddai*, is one of the names of the God of Israel. It means "The Power," or "The God that cannot be obstructed." Thus the common translation, the *Almighty*.

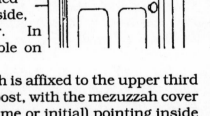

In Hebrew, *Shaddai* is written with the letters, *sheen, dalet, yod.* These letters also serve as an acronym for "*Shomer D'latot Yisrael*," meaning *Protector of the doors of Yisrael*.

Mezuzzah scrolls have the Name *Shaddai* printed on the back (shown above) and are rolled up with Scripture verses inside, then placed inside the cover. In this way, the *Shaddai* is visible on the rolled scroll.

Traditionally, the mezuzzah is affixed to the upper third right-hand portion of the doorpost, with the mezuzzah cover and the top of the Shaddai (name or initial) pointing inside the home at a slight angle of 30 degrees.[16] (See picture.)

The Mezuzzah and our Confession

Our Father instructed us to post His commandments on our doorposts as a witness to the world of our love for Him. Yeshua, said, "Everyone therefore who shall confess Me before men, I will also confess him before My Father who is in Heaven" (Matthew 10:32). And, "I and the Father are One" (John 10:30).

---

16 The *Jewish Book of Why*, by Alfred J. Kolatch, Middle Village, NY: Jonathan David, 1981, 1995, pp 113-16, 151.

We who love the Son also love the Father, and out of love for Him we heed the instructions to post the Law on our doorposts.

We do this because we are blessed when we confess our God before the world. Further, this is the method the Father said we should use to declare to the world that our homes belong to Him.

So delight in, celebrate, enjoy this ancient custom that has so long been upheld by our Jewish brothers.

A Home Dedication Celebration

Have a Home Dedication Celebration and personalize it to fit your family.

For example, you may want to gather with your family to pray and then make a declaration like the Israelites made to Joshua, and which Joshua made to Israel.

The Israelites said to Joshua, "We will serve YHVH our God and listen to His voice."

Joshua responded, "Choose for yourselves today whom you will serve: the gods which your fathers served which were beyond the River, or the gods of the Amorites in whose land you are living. But, as for me and my house, we will serve YHVH" (Joshua 24:15,24).

You can actually write the verses from Deuteronomy on a "scroll" yourself and have your children participate. Simply write them on a single piece of paper, then keep reducing the paper on a copy machine until it is at a workable size.

Mezuzzah covers can be ordered from Messianic Israel Ministries, or you may find them for sale at your local Jewish or Christian bookstore, or on the Internet. A wide variety of styles is available.

To make your home dedication even more special, create your own mezuzzah cover. If your doorway is covered from the elements, the rolled up soft bark of a tree will work well, or you can design one out of clay or tin. Use your imagination.

You may want to anoint (the word actually means to *dedicate*) your home with oil for service, just as Moses anointed the Tabernacle (Leviticus 8:10). Anoint your doorpost with oil and pray the previously suggested prayers that your home might be covered in the Blood of Yeshua.

Another suggested prayer of dedication is:

"Father, may our home be a meeting place for the *wise*" (see Daniel 12:3,9).[17]

Dedicate your home and ask the Father to make it a haven from the wrong influences of the world. Then declare that your home will be a place wherein the song of YHVH is always found. Wonderful music by Lenny and Varda about the restoration of the two houses of Israel is available from Messianic Israel Ministries.

The constant sound of praise music in your home is a sure invitation to the Father's heavenly hosts. So dedicate (or rededicate) your home to the Father.

May He bless your home with His Glorious Presence.

The Mezuzzah

A mezuzzah attached the doorpost of your home can serve as a personal confession that:

♦ You love YHVH with all your heart (Deuteronomy 6:5).

♦ His Living Word/Torah (Yeshua) lives in your heart (Deuteronomy 6:6).

♦ You are teaching His Word to your children (Deuteronomy 6:7).

♦ You look to the Holy One of Israel for all your needs (Deuteronomy 11:14-15).

---

17 The Angel told Daniel that his word was "sealed" until the end time; and that in the end time, "Those who have *insight* will shine brightly like the brightness of the expanse of heaven" (Daniel 12:3,9). This insight speaks of circumspect intelligence, or watchful, detailed, discerning understanding (see *wise*, Strong's word # H7919). In this end time era, let us ask our Father to "unseal" this type of "insight" for us, to bless our homes, and to use them for the gathering of such insightful people.

Pesach Pictures

The Father's feasts are so replete with pictures that instruct us, no one individual can explain them all. For example, instructions for commemorating the Passover were given in Exodus 12:1-27, and in these verses we see that the month of Passover is to be the beginning of months for us. Similarly, receiving Yeshua into our lives marks the beginning of our new life in Him.

Guidelines for Interpreting Scripture Types

To establish a principle for interpreting Scripture types and shadows we quote from *The Feasts of the Lord*, by Robert Thompson, who provides some excellent guidelines.

"Let us mention two rules for interpreting Bible symbols, or types, as they are called. Types, such as the Levitical convocations, help us to understand the Lord Jesus and His plan of salvation.

"The first rule of interpretation is this: study the symbol, and then ask the Holy Spirit to cause the main truth to rise to the surface. Do not focus too long on the details of the symbol and attempt to force the interpretation. You will get sidetracked. We see Bible truth through a glass darkly, as

Paul says in 1 Corinthians 13, and the Holy Spirit must be the One to throw light on the subject. Usually a type presents one main truth, or line of truth, and the Spirit will give us the understanding.

"*For example, Christ is the Lamb of God. The truth which rises to the surface is that Christ was led away as an offering for our sins, and that we eat His body and drink His precious blood as our Passover. But we can't pursue the symbol further and claim that Christ today is led around helplessly and is a prey for every wolf who appears on the scene. Again, in one setting leaven is a type of sin; in another setting leaven is a type of the kingdom of heaven.*

"*Still another example is this: the Christian church is referred to as the bride of the Lamb. This symbol of marriage indicates to us that we enter into spiritual union with Christ, and are made one with Him. But we can't go on from this and state that Christians are feminine because they are called the 'bride,' and that the bride is a different group from the sons of God who are male because they are 'sons.'*"[18]

Three Stages of Progression

The feasts equate symbolically with the layout of the Temple, which had an Outer Court, an Inner Court, and a Holy Place.

The feasts are also divided into three segments: Early Spring, Late Spring, and Fall. These depict the Father's three phase plan of redemption for His people:

Passover (personal redemption), Shavuot/Pentecost (infilling of the Spirit), and Tabernacles (full restoration of Israel's Kingdom).

In these two types, we see divisions of three, as well as three stages of progression. We also know that John the apostle spoke of *children, young men,* and *fathers.* He told the children that their sins were forgiven, he said the young

18 *The Feasts of the Lord,* Robert Thompson, Medford, OR: Omega Publications, 1975, pp 11-12.

men who had overcome the wicked one were strong and that the word of God abides in them. Twice in these same verses, John addresses the fathers and says they *know* the Father (1 John 2:12-14).

Forgiveness of sin corresponds to Passover. It can be likened to the first step one takes in their relationship with the Messiah—just as the Outer Court is the first section to be entered when one walked into Israel's ancient Temple.

Being made strong, or filled with power, corresponds to the power poured out on us in our personal Pentecost experience (Acts 1:8). This feast experience is like entering into the Inner Court of the Temple.

These two feasts speak of what Yeshua accomplished during His sojourn on earth, and they depict our early experiences as Believers.

The Fall feasts, which once foretold that Yeshua would come to tabernacle with His people, now foretell His return to forever dwell with us. These latter feasts also reveal that prior to His return, a work needs to be done by the mature *fathers* in Israel (1 Corinthians 4:15). These Fall feasts foretell the Father's plan to restore all Israel. It is a plan that is precious to His heart. It is plan that is revealed in the Holy Place.

Imagine yourself as a little child who runs into the Holy place and climbs into your Father's lap. You lay your head on His chest and quietly listen to the beat of His heart. This heartbeat is like that of the father of the prodigal, who longed for the return of his lost son and for the reunion of his whole house—both his sons. This is the desire of our Heavenly Father.

The Fall feasts of Israel foretell this reunion. It is a reunion that will be effected by the mature.

May we be granted the grace to be part of that restoration.

The Three Stages of Progression		
Outer Court	Inner Court	Holy Place
Passover	Pentecost	Tabernacles
Children	Young Men	Fathers

Covered With The Blood

The Hebrew word *Pesach* is taken from a word that means to pass, or hover over.[19] This word teaches us that when we are covered by the Blood of Messiah Yeshua, the angel of the second death will "pass over" us (Revelation 2:11; 20:6,14; 218). It tells us that the Holy One will hover, and protect us from evil; He will even cause it to skip over our blood-covered houses (Deuteronomy 32:11; Ezekiel 10:19; 11:22).

Passover teaches us that there is no atonement for sin apart from the shedding of blood (Hebrews 9:22). For this reason our Father told us to put the blood of the lamb on the doorposts of our houses, and then to go in and partake of the lamb. This symbolizes protection; it reveals that even in difficult times there will be houses in which the Father will provide for us.

"None of you shall go outside the door of his house until morning." This verse reveals that no matter how dark the night, there will be a "morning," and "joy" will come with it. Though it was dark in Egypt, there was light in Goshen where His people lived (Exodus 8:22; 10:23). Similarly, we have a "lamp that shines in a dark place." That lamp is Yeshua, the "Morning star." And He will not allow the destroyer to enter into our homes.[20] We can put His Blood on our doorposts, then go in and shut the door behind us, knowing that all will be well and that we only have to celebrate our Passover and wait until morning.

---

19 *Strong's* # H6453. peh'-sakh; from H6452, *paw-sakh*; meaning to hop, skip over (or spare), to hesitate; dance, leap, or pass over.
20 Exo 12:7,22-23; Psa 30:5; 1 Pet. 1:19.

The head of each household had to slay a lamb and sprinkle its blood on the door's lintel and two side posts. Then the lamb was to be roasted with fire and eaten with bitter herbs and unleavened bread. The Israelites were to eat in haste and be dressed and ready to leave Egypt. Their exodus from slavery would begin that night. The angel of death would pass through Egypt and judge every house that did not have the required blood covering.

The lambs that were selected had to be without blemish, and Yeshua, the Lamb of God (John 1:29), was without spot or blemish (1 Peter 1:19). The blood of the lamb was to be applied to the doorposts, and we who believe in the Messiah are of the house of God (Ephesians 2:19; 1 Timothy 3:15; Hebrews 3:6; 1 Peter 2:5). We enter this spiritual house through He Who says, "I say to you, I am the door of the sheep....if anyone enters through Me, he will be saved, and will go in and out and find pasture" (John 10:7-9). We enter through the shed blood of Yeshua .[21]

Partaking of The Lamb

The lamb was to be eaten with unleavened bread, and we are to live unleavened lives in Messiah Yeshua (1 Corinthians 5:6-8; Leviticus 11:44; 19:2; 1 Peter 1:15-16).

The lamb was to be roasted with fire and eaten with bitter herbs. Fire depicts purification, and once we come to know the Lamb, we are tested by fire. We are purified (Zechariah 13:9; James 1:12; 1 Peter 1:7; Revelation 3:18).

Bitter herbs represent the bondage of this world, which is a type of Egypt. Bondage, burdens, and bitterness come when we yield to wickedness. This is true whether the works are those of Satan or of our own doing.[22]

Israel was told, "Now you shall eat it in this manner: with your loins girded, your sandals on your feet, and your staff in your hand; and you shall eat it in haste—it is the

---

21 *The Seven Festivals of the Messiah* by Eddie Chumney, www.geocities. com/Heartland/2175/chap3.
22 *Ibid.*

Lord's Passover" (Exodus 12:11).

The lamb was to be eaten in haste; we must not harden our hearts nor delay when we hear about the Lamb, Yeshua. When He says to us, "Take, eat; this is My body," when we hear Him calling us to drink of the cup of His New Covenant Passover, we must be quick to respond. We must be hasty to leave behind the things of this world and to follow Him alone (1 Samuel 6:6; Psalms 95:8; Hebrews 3:8,5; 4:7; Matthew 4:19; 26:26-28).

Our forefathers had to be girded and shod. Similarly, our loins must be girded with a spirit of servanthood and our feet shod with the gospel of the restored Kingdom (Matthew 24:14; Luke 12:37; 16:16; Romans 10:15; Ephesians 6:14-15).

Taking Up the Staff of Reunion

In addition to being girded and shod, our forefathers were to have a *staff* in their hand. A staff, or *maqqel*, aids us in our walk.[23] Messiah Yeshua sends us the Comforter, the Holy Spirit, the Ruach HaKodesh, to aid and empower us in our walk (John 14:16-26; 15:26; Luke 24:49). Yeshua sent this Helper because the first steps of Passover lead to Unleavened Bread, which is a call to walk in blamelessness, and we cannot walk in that absolute purity unless we are Divinely empowered.

Zechariah spoke of two staffs, when, after Judah's return from Babylon (around 520 B.C.), he said, "I pastured the flock doomed to slaughter....and I took for myself two staffs: the one I called Favor and the other I called Union; so I pastured the flock....[and] I took my staff Favor and cut it in pieces, to break my covenant which I had made with all the peoples ....Then I cut in pieces my second staff Union, to break the brotherhood between Judah and Israel" (Zechariah 11:7-14)

Though the shepherd David once prayed for the Father's

---

23 *Strong's* word # H4731. mak-kale'; to germinate; a shoot, stick (with leaves, or for walking, striking, guiding, divining); rod, staff.

favor to be on all Israel, her errant sons turned the beauty of being favored into false pride. So YHVH gave them into the hands of foreigners, that they might be profaned.[24]

Of Zechariah's staff called Union, the *New International Version Study Bible* says his action is "signifying the dissolution of...the unity between the south and the north."[25] *The Twelve Prophets* calls the staff "Binders" and says, "The ...staff Binders, is now shattered, denoting the dissolution of all unity and harmony between Israel and Judah." [26]

Unity and harmony were taken from Israel and Judah. The staff that bound them together was broken, so each was free to walk in their own way. Because their house is now divided, they cannot stand. They can only stumble along in their limited and separate walks (Luke 11:17; Isaiah 8:14; Romans 11:25).

This same word for staff is used in Jeremiah 1:11-12. There, the Father asked, "What do you see, Jeremiah?" The prophet answered, "I see a rod of an almond tree." To this, the Father replied, "You have seen well, for I am watching over My word to perform it."

An almond branch is known for its ability to *quickly* blossom forth, and Yeshua is about to do a *quick* work in the earth (Revelation 22:7). We who see the truth about the reunion of the two sticks of Ephraim and Judah (as foretold by Ezekiel) must take up this end time Passover staff. We must show forth the staff of good shepherds who truly feed the flock of scattered Israel (Ezekiel 34).

Then we will truly be empowered in our walk, just as the Father promised through Zechariah: *"I will strengthen the house of Judah, and I will save the house of Joseph, and I will bring them back, because I have had compassion on them; and they will be as though I had not rejected them,*

---

24 Psa 90:17; Eze 7:20-22; 24:21; Dan 9:26; Luke 21:5-6.

25 520 B.C.: *New International Version Study Bible, Introduction,* Grand Rapids: Zondervan, 1995, Zechariah, p 1405; NIV quote (same Bible), Zechariah 11:14 footnote, p 1412. Also see "Binders," *The Twelve Prophets,* London: Soncino, 1980, p 267.

26 *The Twelve Prophets,* London: Soncino, 1980, pp 316-317.

Passover in all its Fullness

For I am YHVH their God and I will answer them. Ephraim will be like a mighty man, and their heart will be glad as if from wine; indeed, their children will see it and be glad, their heart will rejoice in YHVH. I will whistle for them to gather them together, for I have redeemed them; and they will be as numerous as they were before. When I scatter them among the peoples, they will remember Me in far countries, and they with their children will live and come back. I will bring them back from the land of Egypt and gather them from Assyria; and I will bring them into the land of Gilead and Lebanon, until no room can be found for them....And I will strengthen them in YHVH, and in His name they will walk,' declares YHVH" (Zechariah 10:6-12).

When the two houses of Israel both humble themselves and begin to seek true reunion, then the fires of revival will spread quickly throughout the world.

We who understand these things must take this end time Passover staff of Favor and Union into our hands.

Chag HaMatzah
The Feast of Unleavened Bread

Our Father instructed Israel to sacrifice their Passover lambs on Abib/Nisan 14.[27] They were to do this at twilight, which begins at the ninth hour of the day, at 3:00 p.m. This was the exact hour when Yeshua was sacrificed for us (Mark 15:33-37).

At that time they could begin roasting their lambs, which would take several hours.

To understand Passover, we must remember that in Hebraic thought the day begins in the evening, at sunset (Genesis 1:5)—which usually happens around 6pm. We must also remember that this Passover day of sacrifice was immediately followed by a seven day period called the Feast of Unleavened Bread, or *Chag HaMatzah,* which begins on Abib 15. In other words, the first actual "day" of Unleavened Bread started before the Israelites could finish roasting their lambs, so the lamb was eaten with unleavened bread.

Of this week long feast, the Father said, "Seven days

---

27 The month of Abib became known as Nisan after the Jews returned from their Babylonian captivity.

you shall eat unleavened bread, but on the first day you shall remove leaven from your houses; for whoever eats anything leavened from the first day until the seventh day, that person shall be cut off from Israel" (Exodus 12:15-20).

For seven days leaven was not allowed in Israel's houses or territories. *Leaven* speaks of sin, and *seven* speaks of the Creation, of rest, spirituality, and perfection.[28] In this feast we see our call to walk in purity. It is a call, as Paul the apostle said, to "Celebrate the feast, not with old leaven, nor with the leaven of malice and wickedness, but with the unleavened bread of sincerity and truth" (1 Corinthians 5:8).

The Feast of Unleavened Bread reminds us of the swift departure our forefathers made from Egypt. They had to leave so quickly they did not have time to put leaven into their bread and wait for it to rise.

When bread rises, it "puffs up," and when we are puffed up with pride or self-focus, our desires are not upright. Too much focus on head knowledge can make people proud, puffed up, arrogant, and unspiritual (Habakkuk 2:4, 1 Corinthians 8:1; Colossians 2:18, NIV).

Unleavened bread depicts our Messiah. Unleavened by life, He was the perfect sacrifice for our sins. Moreover, His body was in the grave during the first days of this feast. He lay there, like a Seed divinely planted, waiting to burst forth as the eternal bread of life.

Yeshua says of Himself, "I am the bread of life; he who comes to Me will not hunger." Yeshua comes to feed hungry souls with the Bread of Life: "This is the bread which comes down out of heaven, so that one may eat of it and not die" (John 6:35,50).

Yeshua was even born in the "house of bread." The Hebrew name of His birth place, *Bethlehem*, is derived from *beit* and *lechem*. *Beit* means *house*, and *lechem* means *bread.*[29]

---

28 *The Wisdom In The Hebrew Alphabet*, Scherman and Zlotowitz, Brooklyn: *ArtScroll Mesorah Series*, 1983, pp 207-210.

29 *Strong's* words # H1035, 1004, 3899.

The Pattern Fulfilled

The Passover lamb was slain on the fourteenth of Abib, and the next day, on the feast of Unleavened Bread, our forefathers left Egypt. Fifty days after the Day of First Fruits, on the Feast of Weeks (Shavuot), the Father gave them the Ten Commandments.

Similarly, Messiah Yeshua was crucified on the fourteenth of Abib (Passover), was in the tomb on the fifteenth (Unleavened Bread), and after three days was resurrected in fulfillment of First Fruits. Fifty days later, the Ruach HaKodesh, He Who fills us with the Living Torah, was poured out on the Believers gathered in Jerusalem for Pentecost (Shavuot).

Chag HaMatzah in Scripture

The Feast of Unleavened Bread, or *Chag HaMatzah*, which is a Sabbath, is explained in Exodus and Leviticus:

"'Moreover, they shall take some of the blood and put it on the two doorposts and on the lintel of the houses in which they eat it. They shall eat the flesh that same night, roasted with fire, and they shall eat it with unleavened bread and bitter herbs....Now this day will be a memorial to you, and you shall celebrate it as a feast to YHVH; throughout your generations you are to celebrate it as a permanent ordinance. 'Seven days you shall eat unleavened bread, but on the first day you shall remove leaven from your houses; for whoever eats anything leavened from the first day until the seventh day, that person shall be cut off from Israel. On the first day you shall have a holy assembly, and another holy assembly on the seventh day; no work at all shall be done on them, except what must be eaten by every person, that alone may be prepared by you (Exodus 12:7-8,14-17).

"You shall also observe the feast of unleavened bread, for on this very day I brought your hosts out of the land of Egypt; therefore you shall observe this day throughout your

generations as a permanent ordinance. On the fifteenth day of the same month there is the feast of unleavened bread to YHVH; for seven days you shall eat unleavened bread. On the first day you shall have a holy convocation; you shall not do any laborious work"(Leviticus 23:6-7).

Unleavened from Sabbath to Sabbath

The Feast of Unleavened Bread has two Sabbaths in it. We are to have a holy assembly on the first and the seventh day. During the week we are to consume no leaven. This command depicts our call to be pure from Sabbath to Sabbath. We are not to put on a spiritual face for our assemblies, then have a different face for friends and families. Peter the apostle , in quoting the Torah, said, "Be ye holy, for I am holy" (1 Peter 1:16, KJV). Week to week, day in and day out, we are called to be unleavened.

Messiah suffered for us and was an example for us. "He committed no sin, nor was any deceit found in his mouth. When being reviled, He did not revile in return; while suffering, He uttered no threats, but kept entrusting Himself to Him who judges righteously." This Sinless One bore our sins in His body on the tree, or cross, so that we might die to sin and live to righteousness. By His wounds we are healed (Isaiah 53:5 1 Peter 2:21-24;).

We are called to follow in Yeshua's righteous footsteps.

Lots of Leaven...

There are many types of leaven in Scripture, all of which can affect Believers. There is the leaven of the Pharisees and the Sadducees, which often depicts hypocrisy, dead ritualism, disbelief, and humanism. There is the leaven of worldliness and sensuality that was displayed in the Corinthians, and the leaven of legalism and pride so prevalent among the Galatians.[30]

---

30 See Mat 2:7-12; 16:5-12; 23:1-3;27-28; Mark 6:14-18; 8:14-15; Luke 11:37-44; 12:1; 1 Cor 4:17-21; 5:1-13; 6:1,9-18; 8:1; 13:4; 2 Cor 12:20-21; Gal
(continued...)

We must not be like these examples, but must keep the feasts in sincerity and truth. To do so, we must be dedicated to our Father and to His purposes in the earth. As Joshua first said, and as Paul the apostle later confirmed, We must "fear [revere] YHVH and serve Him in sincerity and truth" (Joshua 24:14; 1 Corinthians 5:7-8).

Bedikat Chametz

In a previous chapter we explained the Jewish tradition of cleaning the house of leaven, or *Bedikat Chametz* (see *The Father's Passover Plan*). In this tradition, the wife thoroughly cleans the house and removes all leaven, but she deliberately leaves behind some leaven, such as bread crumbs, for the children to find. The father then leads them in a candlelight search for leaven using a feather to brush the leaven onto a wooden spoon, then dropping it into a paper bag. The paper bag filled with the leaven is then discarded or burned.

Because we are of the house of God,[31] our house is to be cleansed of all sin: "Do you not know that you are a temple of God and that the Spirit of God dwells in you?" (1 Corinthians 3:16-19). Also, the Father's Word is a lamp: "Thy word is a lamp unto my feet, and a light unto my path" (Psalm 119:105). In this search for leaven, the candle can be said to represent the Word, and the feather represents the Holy Spirit. We must ask the *Ruach*, the Word of Truth, to reveal our sins and to cleanse our hearts and lives (Ephesians 5:26).

Though traditional Judaism would not agree with the idea, the wooden spoon can be said to represent the tree on which Yeshua was crucified (Deuteronomy 21:22-23). In the ceremony, the leaven was swept onto the spoon, and our

---

30 (...continued)
5:9; 1 John 2:16. Adapted from *The Passover Feast*, Ruth Spector Lascelle, Van Nuys, CA: 1975, p 7; *Pesach and Hag HaMatzah*, Barney Kasdan www.imja.com /maoz; and *The Seven Festivals of the Messiah*, Eddie Chumney, www.geocities. com/Heartland/2175/chap3.

31 Eph 2:19; 1 Tim 3:15; Heb 3:6; 1 Peter 2:5.

sins were put on Yeshua when He died for us on the tree
(Isaiah 53; Romans 5:8; 2 Corinthians 5:21; 1 Thessa-
lonians 5:9-10).

The leaven is burned, which depicts the price to be paid
for sin (Ephesians 4:8-10; Luke 16:19-24).

This hide and seek type search is one that Believers in
Messiah can use to teach their children the good news of
the gospel, as well as the fundamentals of Israel's feasts.

Yom HaBikkurim
The Day of First Fruits

We need to remember a most important "Festival of Joy."

When Believers begin to discover the errors found in Church theology concerning Easter, very often they turn to Judaism. They turn away from anything that has to do with Easter and replace it with a celebration of some form of the Jewish Passover tradition.[32]

However, these worthy Jewish traditions are based on commemoration of our Passover deliverance from Egypt, and on the slaying of a lamb, but we who follow Messiah have something *more* to celebrate. He fulfills this feast, and as our "Passover Lamb," He *arose* from the grave. He came forth as a type of "First of First Fruits," and thus He is "the beginning, the firstborn from the dead" (Colossians 1:18).

If we look through the lens of mercy, we will see that the Christian celebration of the Resurrection, *apart from its errant traditions*, is a type of "First Fruits" celebration.

We do not say this to encourage anything that has to do

---

32 See footnote #3, page 2.

with the ancient pagan cult of "Ishtar," from which the word "Easter" is derived,[33] nor do we want to encourage a parade of bunnies with baskets of colored eggs. Rabbits and eggs are fertility symbols, and Ishtar was the ancient Assyrian/Babylonian goddess of love, fertility, and war.[34]

We say this because Messiah's Resurrection is an event that is *worthy of celebration*. His resurrection from the dead marks a pivotal point in history.

Yeshua is the substance of the day of the sheaf. He is the essence of the first of the first fruits offering that followed Passover. In His resurrection He was the first of the first fruits of resurrection. He "has been raised from the dead the first fruits of those who are asleep" (1 Corinthians 15:20,23).

As our High Priest He was presented before the Father: "He entered through the greater and more perfect tabernacle, not made with hands, that is to say, not of this creation; for Messiah did not enter a holy place made with hands, a mere copy of the true one, but into heaven itself, to appear in the presence of God for us" (Hebrews 9:11,24).

Yeshua's resurrection is a type of harvest. It marked the beginning of our Father's harvest season. Yeshua is "the firstborn among many brethren," and we, His brethren, "also have the first fruits of the Spirit." For this reason we "groan within ourselves"—because we are "waiting eagerly for our adoption as sons, [which is] the redemption of our body." Messiah Yeshua "brought us forth...that we would be a kind of first fruits among His creatures" (Romans 8:29,23; James 1:18).

As we return to our roots we would do well to remember this special day that speaks of mankind's greatest hope. However, we must learn to celebrate it based on its shadow beginning, as described in Torah (Leviticus 23:10-15; Colossians 2:17; Hebrews 10:1).

---

33 The *American Heritage Electronic Dictionary*, Houghton Mifflin, 1994, says the third meaning of Easter is "from Old English *ēastre*, Easter, from Germanic *austrō-*, a dawn-goddess whose holiday was celebrated at the vernal equinox."

34 *Ibid*, "Ishtar."

A "Forgotten" Feast

On the Day of First Fruits, in ancient Israel, the priest waved a sheaf of the first fruits of the barley harvest before the Almighty. Today this feast is largely ignored by most of traditional Judaism. Judah does not celebrate this feast, but Ephraim does, though in an errant way.

Barley Sheaf Offering

Called *Yom HaBikkurim*, or *Day of the First Fruits*, we have much to learn about this most important day.

The word *bikkurim* is plural for *bikkur*, and speaks of the first ripe fruits of the crop. It especially refers to the first products of grain (bread) and fruits.[35]

Israel could not keep this feast until they entered into the Promised Land. They did not keep it in the wilderness where they ate only the manna from heaven. They ceased to eat manna after they had their first Passover, then they ate of the produce of the Land (Joshua 5:10-12).

Yom HaBikkurim is outlined in Leviticus 23:10-15:

"Speak to the sons of Israel and say to them, 'When you enter the land which I am going to give to you and reap its harvest, then you shall bring in the sheaf of the first fruits of your harvest to the priest. 'He shall wave the sheaf before YHVH for you to be accepted; on the day after the sabbath the priest shall wave it. Now on the day when you wave the sheaf, you shall offer a male lamb one year old without defect for a burnt offering to YHVH. Its grain offering shall then be two-tenths of an ephah of fine flour mixed with oil, an offering by fire to YHVH for a soothing aroma, with its drink offering, a fourth of a hin of wine. Until this same day, until you have brought in the offering of your God, you shall eat neither bread nor roasted grain nor new growth.

---

35 *Strong's* H1061, from 1069. bakar; to burst the womb, i.e. (caus.) bear or make early fruit (of woman or tree).; also to give the birthright:--make firstborn, be firstling, bring forth first child (new fruit). Bikkurim: See ; Exo 23:16; 2:1; Lev 2:14; 23:17; Num 13:20; 18:12,13; 2 Ki 4:42; Nah 3:12.

It is to be a perpetual statute throughout your generations in all your dwelling places. You shall also count for your-selves from the day after the sabbath, from the day when you brought in the sheaf of the wave offering; there shall be seven complete sabbaths."

Fulfilled by a Single Priest...

The picture painted by this feast is that of a priest standing alone and waving a sheaf before the Lord. It is a picture of our Messiah, Who is a priest according to the order of Melchizedek" (Hebrews 7:17).

This single priest, who alone made the proper offering, portrays Yeshua, just as does the single sheaf being waved, for Yeshua is "Messiah the First Fruits" (1 Corinthians 15:23).

This first fruit offering was to be waved "on the day after the Sabbath," meaning on the first day of the week, which corresponds to Sunday. This lone priest, who presented an offering to the Father on this day, depicts Yeshua, Who rose from the dead on the first day of the week (Luke 24:1).

Sheaves in Scripture

The first time we read of a *sheaf* in Scripture is in Joseph's dream. In this dream he saw eleven sheaves bow down before his sheaf.[36] The sheaves represented his brothers, who would ultimately bow before him (Genesis 37:5-11; 43:28).

In Scripture, sheaves (plural) can represent a person or persons. A literal sheaf speaks of a pile tied together.

The sheaf that was to be presented on Yom HaBikkurim was called an *omer*. This word comes from *amar*, which is defined as to chastise, as if piling blows, to gather grain and bind sheaves together.[37] An *omer* is a unit of dry measure equal to a tenth of an ephah (Exodus 16:36), which equals about 3.5 liters, or 3.7 quarts.

---

36 *Strong's* #'s H485 and 481, 'alummah, something bound; a sheaf. H481: 'alam, to tie fast; hence, to be tongue-tied: bind, be dumb, put to silence.
37 Omer: *Strong's* #'s H 6016, 6014.

Once more we see a shadow of our High Priest, Yeshua, in that "the chastening for our well-being fell upon Him" (Isaiah 53:5).

We also see a spirit of giving, for Israel was commanded to leave the occasional forgotten sheaf and the gleanings of the harvest in the corners of their fields so they could be used to feed the stranger, the fatherless, the widow and the poor. To do anything less would stop the flow of blessing from YHVH's hand. This principle taught the children of Israel that the joy of harvest should be expressed in charity to others (Leviticus 19:9,22; Deuteronomy 24:19-22; Ruth 2:7,15, 2:15; Job 24:10).

The Barley Sheaf

The sheaf waved on First Fruits was a barley sheaf. On the first day of the week following the regular Sabbath during Unleavened Bread, the harvest of this cereal grain began.

Sown in the winter, barley was the first grain to ripen in the spring. Because of its deep roots, it has a tremendous ability to absorb nutrients from the soil, so it gives a healthy boost to those who eat it.[38]

Similarly, we who have received Messiah Yeshua as Lord are to be firmly rooted in Him, that we might be built up, healthy, established in our faith (Colossians 2:67).[39]

We Are a First Fruits Company

"But now Messiah has been raised from the dead, the first fruits of those who are asleep" (1 Corinthians 15:20). "And not only this, but also we ourselves, **having the first**

---

38   Barley is said to contain all the vitamins, minerals, and proteins necessary for the human diet, and it is thought to give instant access to vital nutrients. See <http://www.aimforenergy.com/barleygreen/bgrass.htm> and <http://www.aim4betterhealthnaturally.com/morabbar.html>

39 *Strong's* # H485: 'alummah, al-oom-maw'; or (masc.) 'alum, aw-loom'.

fruits of the Spirit, even we ourselves groan within ourselves, waiting eagerly for our adoption as sons, the redemption of our body" (Romans 8:23).[40] "But each in his own order: Messiah the first fruits, after that those who are Messiah's at His coming" (1 Corinthians 15:23). For, "In the exercise of His will He brought us forth by the word of truth, so that we would be a kind of first fruits among His creatures" (James 1:18).

Messiah Yeshua is the first of a first fruit company. "He is also head of the body, the ekklesia/congregation; and He is the beginning, the firstborn from the dead, so that He Himself will come to have first place in everything" (Colossians 1:18). By reason of His resurrection from the dead, He was the first to proclaim light, to light the way (Acts 26:23). When we are illumined by His Spirit, we are called "to the general assembly and *ekklesia*/congregation of the firstborn who are enrolled in heaven, and to God, the Judge of all, and to the spirits of the righteous made perfect" (Hebrews 12:23).

Our Messiah is "The first and the last," He died (meaning His earthly flesh ceased to be inhabited by His Spirit), and He "has come to life" (Revelation 2:8). He is our resurrection hope. It is a glorious hope that must not be forgotten, for we who belong to Him will forever live in His presence. So let us rejoice in our First Fruits Priest Who made eternal life possible for us.

The Most Choice

The first fruits were considered the choicest of all. They were consecrated, or holy unto YHVH. The firstborn of man and beast belonged to Him, as did the first fruits of the earth (Exodus 13:2; 11-13, 22:29). However, some of the first fruits were presented to the priests and Levites (Leviticus 19:23-25; Nehemiah 10:34-39). All first fruits were to be offered with thanksgiving and praise.

---

40 The Spirit of adoption is mentioned only five times in Scripture. All must receive it to become sons of God, and it belongs to "the sons of Israel" (Rom 8:15, 23; 9:4; Gal 4:5; Eph 1:5); *Who Is Israel?* chapter 14, "*More Tattered Theories.*"

A List of Firsts

Yeshua fulfills the shadow of First Fruits. He is first in every way. He is given first place in everything, because all things are being summed up in Him. He is all, and can be found in all (Ephesians 1:10-11,23).

Messiah Yeshua is—
♦ The firstborn of the Father (Hebrews 1:6).[41]
♦ The firstborn of every creature (Colossians 1:15).
♦ The firstborn of Mary/Miryam (Matthew 1:23-25).
♦ The firstborn from the dead (Revelation 1:5).
♦ The firstborn of many brethren (Romans 8:29).

Yeshua is the First (*Aleph*) and the Last (*Tav*), the *Alpha* and the *Omega*, the *Beginning* and the *End* (Revelation 1:8,17; 21:6; 22:13; Isaiah 41:4; 44:6; 48:12). "He is also head of the body, the *ekklesia/congregation*, and He is the beginning, the firstborn from the dead, so that He Himself will come to have *first place in everything*. For it was the Father's good pleasure for all the fullness to dwell in Him, and through Him to reconcile all things to Himself, having made peace through the blood of His cross; through Him, I say, whether things on earth or things in heaven" (Colossians 1:18-20).

The Ceremony

To fulfill the First Fruits obligation in ancient Israel, the celebrant would take the first sheaf from his barley harvest to the priest, who would then wave the sheaf before YHVH in the Temple. As it is written, "'He shall wave the sheaf before YHVH for you to be accepted; on the day after the sabbath the priest shall wave it" (Leviticus 23:11).

In the heavens, on the day this feast saw its fulfillment, Yeshua waved a wave sheaf in our behalf. When He offered that holy sheaf, all were accepted—all who *were* His, all who

---

41 Israel is the Father's firstborn, and His "Servant," Who is Yeshua, also is named "Israel" (Exo 4:22; Isa 49:3; Hos 11:1; Mat 2:15,18).

are His, and all who *ever will be* His. "For Messiah did not enter a holy place made with hands...but into heaven itself, to appear in the presence of God for us." And He did this, "Once and for all" (Exodus 25:40; Romans 6:10; Hebrews 7:27; 9:12,24; 10:10).

Counting the Omer

On this day of waving the sheaf, Israel is to begin counting off "seven complete sabbaths." This counting process has come to be known as "counting the omer." The count begins on the Day of First Fruits, and is culminated fifty days later on Shavuot.

For this fifty day interval a special custom arose that Jewish people celebrate to this day. On each of these fifty days a "counting benediction" is recited and days are marked off on a calendar:

Blessed are You, O Lord our God, King of the Universe, Who has sanctified us the Thy commandments, and has commanded us concerning the counting of the omer.

This blessing is followed by saying:

"This is the ___ day, being ___ weeks and ___ days of the omer." [42]

The "Sabbath" Controversy And Why it Matters

There has long been a controversy over how to interpret the command to begin the count on "the day after the Sabbath" (Leviticus 23:11). Some people think this reference to "the Sabbath" refers to the weekly Sabbath. Others think it refers to the first day of Unleavened Bread, which is a "Feast Sabbath." Since Shavuot has no assigned date beyond beginning the count on "the day after the Sabbath," we need to understand which Sabbath is meant in order to know when to celebrate Shavuot.

---

[42] *The Everlasting Tradition*, Galen Peterson, Grand Rapids: Kregal Publications, 1995, pp 28-29.

Sunday to Sunday

If we say the verse speaks of the weekly Sabbath, then the waving of the First Fruits will always be on a Sunday, and Shavuot will always fall on a Sunday—exactly seven Sabbaths plus one day, or fifty days later.

Sabbath versus Shabbaton

The word "Sabbath," which is used in this verse, is the word used to speak of the *weekly* Sabbath. The word used to describe feast days of rest is "*Shabbaton*."[43] The only exception to this rule is Yom HaKippurim, the holiest day of the year. That most holy day is called a Sabbath of complete rest, a *Shabbat Shabbaton*[44]

Restated, the weekly Sabbath can be, and is, sometimes called a *Shabbat Shabbaton* (Exodus 31:15), however, except for Yom HaKippurim. the word *Shabbat* is *not* applied to the feast days. They are days of *Shabbaton.*

Thus it would appear that "the day after the Sabbath" (Leviticus 23:11) would *not* refer to the first day of Unleavened Bread, for that is a *Shabbaton*, a *feast day.* Instead, it refers to the weekly Sabbath.

Moreover, if we were to begin the count on Unleavened Bread, then Shavuot would always fall on the sixth of Sivan (the third month), because the feast of Unleavened Bread begins on a fixed date—the fifteenth of Abib (Leviticus 23:6). Therefore, there would be no need to count the days; we would simply be instructed to observe Shavuot on the sixth of Sivan. (See charts this chapter.)

Calendar Charts

The following calendars count the omer based on the two methods previously discussed.

As you study these calendars, keep in mind that we are solely addressing the issue of the counting of the omer.

---

43 *Strong's* # H7677, from H7676; special holiday; rest, sabbath.
44 www.karaite-korner.org/light-of-israel/pentecost_classical_proofs.shtml

The first calendar is based on the scriptural command that the count begins on the morrow after the *weekly* Sabbath, a Sunday, and it ends on a Sunday, as is required. This is the counting method that we believe is scripturally correct.

The Sabbath mentioned must be the weekly Sabbath, because there are to be "fifty" days and "seven" sabbaths in the counting: "'You shall count fifty[45] days to the day after the seventh sabbath; then you shall present a new grain offering" (Leviticus 23:16).

The second calendar follows the rabbinic assumption that the counting begins after the first day of Unleavened Bread—which is a *Shabbaton*, and not a regular *Sabbath* day. Our example has that day, the fifteenth of Abib, falling on a Thursday. This means their fifty day count ends on a Friday, which is *not* the day after the Sabbath, and the count must end on the day "after" the Sabbath. On that calendar, since they count the first day of Unleavened Bread as a "Sabbath," they have a total of eight Sabbaths in their count.

What First Fruits Means to Us

We celebrate this feast because, for Believers, First Fruits reminds us that our God is the source of all blessings, that we are to seek first His Kingdom, and that He is always to be our first love.[46]

This time of counting the days between the waving of the First Fruits barley sheaf and the harvesting of the wheat is a depiction of our earthly sojourn. For we are strangers and exiles in this earth. Our time here is a time of expectation, a time of knowing that the Father will provide. We know we have a coming inheritance, and we know the final "Ingathering" is coming soon (Hebrews 11:13-14; Acts 26:18; Ephesians 1:11,14,18; Colossians 1:12; 1 Peter 1:4).

Just as we are blessed when we accept Yeshua into our

---

45 *Strong's* # H2572.
46 Mat 6:33; 1 John 4:9; Rev 2:4.

hearts as the Passover Lamb, so there is something more. For Yeshua has made a way for us to enter into Eternity with the Father. We who have repented of our sins and believe in Yeshua have this hope of resurrection. We hope in the coming first fruits harvests.

Celebrating Yom HaBikkurim

One way we can celebrate this awesome day is to take individual sheaves of barley and tie them with colorful ribbons, then gather family and friends and joyously wave our individual barley sheaves before the Father. We can offer Him songs of thanksgiving and praise. Let us remember to be as priests before Him, and like Aaron, bear the burden of all the tribes on our breasts. On this day in particular, we can intercede in prayer for the whole house of Israel.

You also might want to have someone dress as a priest, and others dress as Israelites who are bringing in their sheaves. Someone can read all the appropriate verses while the people act out the feast. Give the children a calendar on which they can begin counting off the days until Shavuot. Pray! Sing! Rejoice! Give gifts! Worship and celebrate on this day that speaks of the Resurrection work of He Who is the First of First Fruits!

Scriptural Counting Method

Counting from the Morrow after the Weekly Sabbath						
Sun	Mon	Tues	Wed	Thurs	Fri	Sabbath
			Abib 14– Passover	Abib 15– 1st day of Un-leavened Bread	Abib 16	
1 Day of First Fruits	2	3	4	5	6	1st Sabbath
8	9	10	11	12	13	2nd Sabbath
15	16	17	18	19	20	3rd Sabbath
22	23	24	25	26	27	4th Sabbath
29	30	31	32	33	34	5th Sabbath
36	37	38	39	40	41	6th Sabbath
43	44	45	46	47	48	7th Sabbath
50 Shavuot= Morrow after the 7th Sabbath						

Rabbinical Counting Method

Counting from the Day of Unleavened Bread						
Sun	Mon	Tues	Wed	Thurs	Fri	Sabbath
			Abib 14– Passover	Abib 15– Day of Un- leavened Bread	Abib 16– [Day of First Fruits?]	2
3	4	5	6	7	8	1st Sabbath
10	11	12	13	14	15	2nd Sabbath
17	18	19	20	21	22	3rd Sabbath
24	25	26	27	28	29	4th Sabbath
31	32	33	34	35	36	5th Sabbath
38	39	40	41	42	43	6th Sabbath
45	46	47	48	49	50 Rabbinic Shavuot	

Passover in all its Fullness

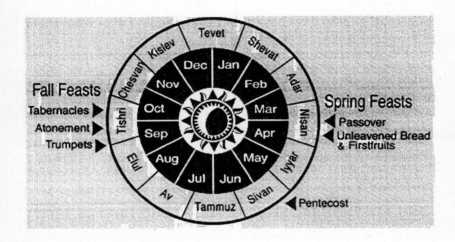

Chart from:
The Holidays of God by Kevin Williams
Martin R. De Haan II, President of RBC Ministries
http://www.gospelcom.net/rbc/ds/q0408/

Addendum A

Traditional and Messianic Jewish Celebrations

For the sake of those not familiar with the Traditional Jewish Passover Haggadah, or the Messianic Jewish Passover celebration, we offer the following information.

Often called the "Festival of Freedom," Passover is a celebration of deliverance from slavery. This feast is the oldest of the appointed feasts of Israel. Like *Sukkot* and *Shavuot*, it required a pilgrimage to Jerusalem.

When our forefather, Joseph, was the second most powerful man in Egypt, his family ultimately joined him there. Generations later there arose another Pharaoh —one who knew not Joseph. With his rise to power the political climate changed. The Hebrew family that once was related to the "Prime-Minister" was reduced to slavery.

Moses was born to a Hebrew slave, but was adopted by Pharaoh's daughter. When he became a man he was overcome when he saw a fellow Hebrew being mistreated, so he intervened, striking and killing the offender. Then, fearing for his life, he fled into the desert.

Much later, at the Father's insistence, a more subdued, yet stronger, Moses returned and demanded the release of the Hebrews from bondage.

So began the Passover battle between Pharaoh and the Holy One—between worldliness and godliness—between bondage and freedom.

After each of Moses' requests for freedom to worship were refused, the God of Israel struck the Egyptians with a different plague. Finally, Moses threatened a tenth plague, one that would kill all the firstborn Egyptian sons and cattle, because they did not have the blood on their doorposts. Pharaoh foolishly refused to obey, so death came to his son. After the Egyptian firstborn were killed by the angel of death, Pharaoh told the Israelites to leave.

Since they were in a rush to depart, there was not even enough time for their bread to rise. So began the Israelite custom of eating unleavened bread, beginning at Passover.[47]

The Telling of the Story

In most Jewish homes, the first night of Passover features a family dinner that includes retelling the Passover story and singing certain songs. It is called a *Seder*, which means *order, because a particular order* is followed. A book called the *Haggadah*, which means *the telling of the story*, outlines the script for this special night. This instruction book can be small or large, plain or ornate, and often is a family heirloom.

The telling of the story, or *Haggadah*, begins when the youngest child asks the traditional question:

"*Why is this night different from all other nights*"?

With this question, the recounting of the story of great redemption begins.

During the course of the evening four cups of wine are offered. These are said to correspond to the Father's four Exodus promises:"I shall bring you forth, I shall save you, I shall redeem you, I shall take you" (Exodus 6:6-7).

---

47 Exo 7:1; 13:22; Luke 22:1.

The names of the four cups recount these promises. They are called the cups of Sanctification, Deliverance, Redemption, and Praise.

Matzoth (unleavened bread) and *maror* (bitter herbs, usually horseradish) are eaten as reminders of the hasty exodus, and of the bitterness of slavery.

Over the years, rabbis have added other elements to the Passover ritual plate: a green vegetable (*karpas*), a roasted egg, *charoset* (finely chopped apples and nuts mixed with honey and wine to resemble the mortar used for the infamous bricks made in Egypt), and a fifth cup of wine: the cup of Elijah. A place is set at the table and the door left open for him. Elijah's cup traditionally sits on the Passover table, waiting for him to come and drink, and to announce that Messiah has come.

During the service, some *charoset* and *maror* are eaten with a piece of *matzah*. Called a "Hillel Sandwich," it is named after the great rabbi, and it is eaten to remind us that even the most bitter of circumstances can be made sweet—if we hold fast to our hope in the God of Israel.

The Traditional Jewish Seder Table

The traditional Jewish Seder table usually includes a large Seder plate (which may be a family treasure). On this plate there is a roasted lamb shank bone, a hard cooked egg, *maror*, the *charoset* mix, and *karpas* (lettuce, parsley, or watercress). Three *matzoth* are kept on the table under a cover, along with salt water to dip the parsley in, as a reminder of the salty tears of slavery. An ornate cup for the wine is also on the table, with two candles that are lit at the beginning of the Seder as a special blessing is recited.

Passover is a time for the people of Israel to teach their children about the wonderful works of God. It is a time to celebrate the history of the people of Israel. For Messiah's followers this is a time to celebrate, because He fulfills Passover. His sacrificial death brings us into a new Exodus that is a departure from our bondage to sin.

The Messianic Jewish Passover Seder

Messianic Jewish Believers claim that Yeshua was following some form of this tradition when He celebrated His New Covenant Passover.

They also teach that some new truths can be seen in their version of the traditional Jewish Seder:

The three *matzoth* commemorate the unleavened bread of affliction that our forebearers ate in their hasty departure. Some believe the First Century Jewish Believers in Messiah used three *matzoth,*, with the middle one representing the Son who was broken for us. They believe this custom spread throughout Judaism and remains today.[48]

The roasted shank bone is said to speak of the spotless lamb sacrificed on the first Passover. When the Holy One saw the blood of this sacrifice, He passed over our people and did not kill the firstborn. Today, Yeshua is our sinless *Paschal* Lamb, sacrificed once for all (Hebrews 7:27; 9:12; 10:10; 1 Peter 3:18). He paid the ultimate price for our redemption, and if we abide in Him, we too will one day be "passed over" by the angel of the second death.

The roasted egg, or *khagigah*, is said to symbolize eternal life, having no beginning nor end, even as our God is without beginning or end.

Maror, the bitter herb, brings to mind the bitterness of slavery in Egypt, as well as the bitterness of slavery to sin.

Charoset, with its Egyptian brick mortar color, reminds us of the backbreaking labor that comes with bondage.

Karpas, a spring-time vegetable, tells of God's rich bounty, of our spring-time deliverance and our hope in Him.

After searching, a child locates the hidden *afikomen* (the broken half of the middle *matzah*), which is then blessed as the Body of Yeshua, who is the Bread of Life.

---

48 *The Book of Jewish Knowledge* by Nathanel Ausubel (NY: Crown Publishers, 1977), says: "This ceremonial custom [the Seder], in imitation of the patrician manner of banqueting customary in Greco-Roman times, began in the first century, when the Seder was introduced..." See "Passover," p 328.

The third cup of wine drunk during this tradition is called the cup of Redemption. After it is blessed, the participants drink what is said to be the wine of the New Covenant, as lifted up by Yeshua during His "Last Supper."

This cup is followed by a fourth cup of wine and the ceremony is concluded. (See *Messianic Jewish Passover Guide* on the following pages.)

What was Yeshua Doing?

Again we ask, was Yeshua following the *Order* of the Passover that was practiced in His day, or was He initiating a new Passover tradition? (See chapter 1, *The Father's Passover Plan.*)

Yeshua spoke against the traditions of men. Paul likewise warned us about being taken captive by errant traditions. Instead, we are to do all things according to the way of the Messiah (Mark 7:6-8; Colossians 2:8). So we again ask: "How did Yeshua celebrate His New Covenant Passover?"

Beyond Tradition

Other than saying we are fairly certain Yeshua did not have a "Passover plate," as we now know them, and that many of the present Jewish traditions have been added over the centuries, and thus are not Biblical commands, we choose not to argue the finer points of Jewish traditions. Instead, we suggest researching the topic with books like, *The Jewish Book of Why, Volumes One and Two* by Alfred J. Kolatch (Jonathan David Publishers, Inc., 68-22 Eliot Avenue, Middle Village, NY, 11379). Kolatch answers many questions about various traditions.

We prefer incorporating the concept of the *Four Passovers*, as earlier described. Nonetheless, we also offer a *Messianic Jewish Passover Guide* for those who wish to celebrate in a more traditional way. We do this because we realize there is much we can learn by experiencing a

Passover in this manner.

All of our *Passover Guides* are offered for sale in the back of this book. You can order a printed copy, or you may photocopy the four copyrighted pages for your personal use.

However you choose to celebrate, may your celebration be blessed with the Messiah's presence.

Messianic Jewish Passover Haggadah

Angus and Batya Wootten
PO Box 700217, Saint Cloud, FL 34770
Ph. 800 829-8777   Fax 407 348-3770
email: info@mim.net   Web: www.mim.net
Ministering to "both the houses of Israel" (Isaiah 8:14)

Pesach: The Festival of Freedom: *Pesach* is a feminine word meaning, to skip over, to pause or hover over, even as a hen hovers over her chicks.

The Search For Leaven: Leaven swells, puffs up, and permeates, it serves as a symbol for sin. On the 13th of Abib, Jewish fathers begin with a ceremonial search for leaven called *bedikat chametz* (Exo 12:15). They lead the children in a candlelight search using a feather, wooden spoon, and rag or bag. The crumbs (some have been knowingly hidden), feather, spoon and rag then are ceremonially burned.

The Haggadah: Haggadah means "the telling, or showing forth." These books often are family heirlooms and are based on answering the "What does this rite mean to you?" question that is to be asked by the youngest child (Exo 12:26-27).

The Seder Table: The table is often adorned with a Menorah and a traditional Passover plate on which we find: a lamb shank-bone, roasted egg, bitter herbs, horseradish, parsley, and *charoset* (mix of chopped apples, nuts, raisins, cinnamon, and wine).

On the table we also find: A dish filled with salt water (for dipping), a wine cup, a cup for Elijah, covers for the *matzoth* (the three pieces of unleavened bread), *afikomen* (half of the one broken and hidden matzoth), and a bowl for washing, with a towel for drying, plus a pillow for leaning. Each of these Passover element pieces may be plain or elaborate.

The Four Cups: According to rabbinic tradition four cups of wine are drunk at the Seder to represent the four expressions of redemption: "I will *free* you," "I will *deliver* you," "I will *redeem* you," "I will *take* you" (Exo 6:6-7). These cups are called: Sanctification, Plagues, Redemption, and Praise.

The Seder (Order):

✿ The head of the house says the *Kiddish* (blessing over the wine) and all drink the first cup of wine, called the cup of *Sanctification.*

✿ The lady of the house takes the bowl around for the washing of the hands.

✿ All dip *karpas* (parsley: a reminder of the *springtime* deliverance) in the salt water (reminder of the tears shed in slavery and of the sea of deliverance), then eat it.

✿ Leader raises the matzah, all recite over the *Bread of Affliction.*

"This is the bread of affliction, the poor bread which our fathers ate in the land of Egypt. Let all who are hungry come and eat. Let all who are in need come and share in the hope of Passover."

✿ Leader breaks the *middle matzah* into two pieces, wraps one half in the *afikomen* bag and then hides it. Later, the children try to find it. Leader *redeems* it from the child who finds it, and they get a reward at *Shavuot* (Pentecost).

✿ The Four Questions are asked by the youngest child:

"On all other nights we eat bread or matzah. On this night *why* do we eat only matzah?

"On all other nights we eat all kinds of vegetables. On this night *why* do we eat only bitter herbs?

"On all other nights we do not dip our vegetables even once. On this night *why* do we dip them twice?

©BRW

"On all other nights we eat our meals sitting or reclining. On this night *why* do we eat only reclining?"

✢ Leader then begins to answer the questions, first explaining and distributing the other half of the broken, "striped and pierced," matzah (Isa 53:5).

✢ All take a piece of matzah with *maror* (horseradish: a reminder of the *bitterness* of slavery in Egypt (Exo 1:12-14)—called a "Hillel Sandwich" after the great rabbi.

✢ Second Dipping: All take a piece of matzoth with *maror*, and dip it into the sweet *charoset* (apple and wine) mix, as a reminder that even the most bitter of circumstances are *sweetened* by hope in our God.

✢ Second cup of wine, *Plagues*, is poured and Leader tells the Passover story. When the ten plagues are recited—blood, frogs, vermin, mixture, pestilence, boils, hail, locusts, darkness, slaying the firstborn—for each plague, a drop of wine (taken from the cup) is sprinkled on the plates. At the end of the story the second cup of wine is drunk.

✢ Leader reclines on pillow, saying, "The first Passover was celebrated by a people enslaved."

✢ All say, "Once we were slaves, but now we are free!"

✢ Leader holds up the *khagigah*, or egg, stating that it reminds us of new birth and eternal life for it has no beginning nor end (may be eaten later with the meal).

✢ The *Dayenu: Dayenu* means, "It would have been sufficient."

Leader: If the Lord had merely rescued us, but had not judged the Egyptians,

All: *Dayenu!*

Leader: If He had only destroyed their gods, but had not parted the Red Sea,

All: *Dayenu!*

Leader: If He had only drowned our enemies, but had not fed us with *manna*,

All: *Dayenu!*

Leader: If He had only led us through the desert, but had not given us the Sabbath,

All: *Dayenu!*

Leader: If He had only given us the Torah, but not the Land of Israel,

All: *Dayenu!*

Leader: But, the Holy One, blessed be He, provided all these things, and many more, for our forefathers—and so He will provide for us—for we are their children!

All: Blesses are You, O Holy One, for You supply all our needs!

✢ It is now time to partake of the Passover Meal

After the meal, the Seder continues...

✿ Leader shares the Afikomen and says: "This is My body which is given for you; do this in remembrance of Me" (Luke 22:19)

✿ The third cup of wine is poured, the cup of *Redemption*. Leader says: "This cup which is poured out for you is the new covenant in My blood" (Lk 22:20).

✿ Lift up Elijah's cup and open the door for him (Mal 4:5; Luke 1:17; Matt 11:14).

✿ Leader pours and lifts up the fourth cup of wine, *Praise,* and says:

Give thanks to the Lord, for He is good.
All: His love endures forever.
Leader: Give thanks to the God of gods.
All: His love endures forever.
Leader: Give thanks to the Lord of Lords.
All: His love endures forever.
Leader: To Him who alone does great wonders,
All: His love endures forever.
Leader: Who by His understanding made the heavens,
All: His love endures forever.
Leader: Who spread out the earth above the waters,
All: His love endures forever.
Leader: Who made the great lights,
All: His love endures forever.
Leader: The sun to govern the day,
All: His love endures forever.
Leader: The moon and stars to govern the night,
All: His love endures forever.
Leader: To Him who struck down the firstborn of Egypt
All: His love endures forever.
Leader: And brought Israel out from their midst,
All: His love endures forever.
Leader: With a strong hand and an outstretched arm,
All: His love endures forever.
Leader: To Him who divided the Red Sea asunder,
All: His love endures forever.
Leader: And brought Israel through the midst of it,
Leader: But He overthrew Pharaoh and his army in the Red Sea,
All: His love endures forever.
Leader: To Him who led His people through the wilderness,
All: His love endures forever.
Leader: Give thanks to the God of Heaven!
All: His love endures forever.

(Psalm 136:1-16,26)

✿ Lift the cup of *Praise* and bless the name of the Lord!
All say: *Next Year In Jerusalem! It Is Finished!*

Addendum B

Paul and the Feasts

Did Paul instruct the non-Jewish Believers not to keep the Law, or did he uphold the Torah?

When Paul wanted Timothy to go with him to the Jewish people, Rabbi Paul circumcised him (Acts 16:1-3). Paul also kept a Nazarite vow and paid for others to keep their vows (Acts 18:18; 21:21-28; see Numbers 6:2,5,9,18). Paul instructed us to keep Passover, and he said, "In my inner being I delight in God's law," and, "I have committed no offense either against the Law of the Jews or against the temple or against Caesar." Paul also said, "The Law is good, if [IF] one uses it **lawfully**" (Acts 20:16; 1 Corinthians 5:8; Romans 7:22; Acts 24:14; 25:8; 1 Timothy 1:8).

Good, or *kalos*, means beautiful, valuable, virtuous, honest, well, worthy. *Lawfully*, or *nomimos*, means legitimately, lawfully, agreeable to the rules.

Paul did not speak against the law or the feasts but against the errant legalisms of men. He said, "The Law is holy...righteous...good...spiritual," and, "It is not the hearers of the Law who are just before God, it is those who obey the law who will be declared righteous" (Romans 7:12,14; 2:13). Paul's detractors had to put forth "*false*" witnesses to try to prove their lie that he spoke "against Moses" (Acts 6:13).

Paul said he served God the way his "forefathers did," and that he "believed everything that is in accordance with the Law." He also spoke of having the Law written on our hearts, and he said that, "All Scripture is inspired by God and profitable for teaching, for reproof, for correction, for training in righteousness; that the man of God may be adequate, equipped for every good work" (Acts 24:14; Romans 2:13-16; 2 Timothy 1:3; 3:16-17).

When Paul said this, he spoke of Old (First) Covenant Scriptures, because the New Covenant was not yet Canon.[49]

Three Primary Verses

There are three primary Scripture verses in the New Covenant that are often said to prove that the feasts should not be celebrated by New Covenant Believers.

These verses are: *Galatians 4:8-11; Colossians 2:16-17; and Romans 14:1-6.*

For more information on these Scriptures than is provided here, with the understanding that the following books were written from a *Messianic Jewish perspective*, we recommend the relevant comments in the *Jewish New Testament Commentary* by David H. Stern, and also those in the book, *Take Hold* by Ariel and D'vorah Berkowitz.

Galatians 4:8-11

"When you did not know God, you were slaves to those which by nature are no gods. But now that you have come to know God, or rather to be known by God, how is it that you turn back again to the weak and worthless elemental things, to which you desire to be enslaved all over again? You observe days and months and seasons and years. I fear for you, that perhaps I have labored over you in vain."

Some people believe the problem with the Galatians was that they thought strict obedience to the Law and

---

49 Note: Torah foretells One Who will speak the words of the Father, and Israel is commanded to listen to Him. Yeshua fulfilled this prophecy and He prayed for those who would believe in Him through the "Words" of His Disciples (Deu 18:18-19; John 5: 46-47; 8:28; 12:49-50; 17:8,17). Thus Torah validates the New Covenant. See, "Has Torah Failed Us? Do We Have The Promised Words of The Prophet?" @ www.mim.net;; Messianic Israel Herald, Vol. 2 No. 2.

circumcision would bring them salvation. According to this theory, Paul feared for them because they had begun to celebrate the Biblical feast days. However, we note that the epistle to the Galatians was written about a situation in Galatia wherein the Judaizers were imposing hard-and-fast legalisms on the non-Jewish Believers. They asserted that an individual could only be saved if they were circumcised and kept the Law to the letter.

However, the truth is that legalism does not result in eternal salvation. Eternal salvation is the result of one being spiritually regenerated through faith in the atoning work of our Messiah, Yeshua.

We define "Judaizers" as those who try to bring people into conformity with Judaism, particularly to adopt rabbinic interpretations of Torah, much of which is based on oral law rather than on written Scripture.

David Stern, a commentator with a decidedly Messianic Jewish slant, says of these verses, "When Gentiles observe these Jewish holidays neither out of joy in sharing what God has given the Jewish people nor out of spiritual identification with them, but out of fear induced by Judaizers who have convinced them that unless they do these things, God will not accept them, then they are not obeying the Torah but subjecting themselves to legalism; and legalism is just another species of **those weak and miserable elemental** demonic **spirits** no better than the idols left behind." [50]

Stern suggests the "days, months, seasons and years" may refer to pagan traditions. This may be so because Paul spoke of those who were once *foreign* to the God of Israel. He said: "You were slaves to those which by nature are no gods," and he asked them, "How is it that you turn back again to the weak and worthless elemental things?"

In the same letter, Paul warns of the "elemental things of the world" (Galatians 4:3). Moreover, he warned the Believers of Colosse, "See to it that no one takes you captive

---

50 *Jewish New Testament Commentary* by David H. Stern, Clarksville, MD: Messianic Jewish Publications, 1995, p 557.

...according to the elementary principles of the world, rather than according to Messiah" (Colossians 2:8).

"Things of the world" does not describe the principals of Messiah, nor the Biblical feasts. The feasts are "YHVH's appointed times" (Leviticus 23:2). These divinely set-apart times are *not* weak and miserable principles.

Paul's admonition can be seen both as a warning against returning to heathen practices *and* against being intimidated by Judaizers.

Paul also said of those who were causing the problem: "They eagerly seek you, not commendably, but they wish to shut you out so that you will seek them" (Galatians 4:17).

Judaizers try to put you in bondage to themselves and to their man-made rules. Their actions are not commend-able, because they try to get you to seek approval from them, so they can feel important by "shutting you out." In other words, they make you feel unworthy and excluded so they can feel good about themselves.

Such attitudes are not godly or edifying.

Colossians 2:16-17

"Let no one act as your judge in regard to food or drink or in respect to a festival or a new moon or a Sabbath day— things which are a mere shadow of what is to come; but the substance belongs to Messiah."

To understand these verses, we need to look back to verse 8, where Paul warned, "See to it that no one takes you captive through philosophy and empty deception, according to the tradition of men, according to the elementary principles of the world, rather than according to Messiah."

Paul was talking about the traditions of men, and he warned us not to be taken in by them.

However, though Paul repeatedly spoke against such deceptions, he was nonetheless a rabbi who honored Torah and continually taught from the *Tanach*, the Old Testament. Our interpretations of his writings must be based on this understanding about the apostle from Tarsus.

The New American Standard Bible adds the word "mere" in italics in verse 17. *Italics* means it is not in the Greek text but the translator feels it is implied.

We find a more accurate translation in the New King James Versions, which tells us that the feasts are "a shadow of things to come, but the substance is of Messiah."

These verses emphasize the truth that the feasts shadow, outline, depict, and portray, our Messiah. Stern puts an even greater emphasis on their connection to Yeshua, saying the verse should be rendered: "These are *definitely* a shadow of things to come." Or: "The festivals do *indeed* have value."

We agree with Stern, because as stated earlier, "shadows cannot be separated from their substance." [51] Moreover, Stern quotes R. C. Lenski, who says, "We should not think lightly of the shadow. It was no less than the divine promise of all the heavenly realities about to arrive."[52]

In these verses, when Paul says to let no one "act as your judge" in these matters, it may be that he was telling the Colossians not to let the *heathen* judge them for "*honoring*" the scriptural feasts, dietary laws, new moon festivals, and the Sabbath (vs 2:16).

We say this because the Jerusalem Council ruled in Acts 15 that the new converts coming to faith were expected to obey certain minimal requirements, as well as go to the synagogue to hear the words of Torah.

Acceptance of these converts might be said to be attached to a "hinge statement." That hinge statement is found in Acts 15:21: "**For Moses from ancient generations has in every city those who preach him, since he is read in the synagogues every Sabbath.**"

Hearing the Torah and having its eternal laws written on our hearts is the very essence of the promised New

51 See *Israel's Feast and their Fullness*, chapter 2, "Where Do We Go For Answers?, and, *Who Is Israel?* chapter 22, "Return, O Virgin Israel!"
52 *Jewish New Testament Commentary*, p 611.

Covenant (Jeremiah 31:31-33). [53]

In other words, these new Believers were being accepted into the fellowships with minimal behavior requirements, *because* it was assumed that they would soon begin to hear and obey the eternal truths taught by Moses.

Looking through this lens, we see that concerning the Colossian verses in question, Paul was declaring that true meaning and fulfillment of the feast shadows are found in the Messiah. From this perspective, we also see that these verses were meant to *encourage* us to celebrate the feasts, because they depict our Messiah to the world. They portray the pattern of His life, His plan of redemption for our lives, and His Second Coming.

The Word tells us, "Now these things happened to them as an example, and they were written for our instruction, upon whom the ends of the ages have come" (1 Corinthians 10:11). Many believe we are possibly the last generation, the one upon whom the ends of the ages have come. If so, to understand YHVH's redemptive plan for humanity, we need to honor our Messiah in the holy days that He set apart for us. They will help us to better understand that which is to happen in the earth. His orderly appointed times help us to understand His prophetic plan.

Just as it could be that the *heathen* were judging the Believers of Colosse for "honoring" the scriptural feasts, so it could be that the *Judaizers* were judging or condemning them for not following their rabbinic teachings.

Romans 14:1-6

"Now accept the one who is weak in faith, but not for the purpose of passing judgment on his opinions. One person has faith that he may eat all things, but he who is weak eats vegetables only. The one who eats is not to regard with contempt the one who does not eat, and the one who does not eat is not to judge the one who eats, for God

---

53 *Who Is Israel?* by Batya Wootten, chapter 19, "One Law—One People."

has accepted him. Who are you to judge the servant of another? To his own master he stands or falls; and he will stand, for the Lord is able to make him stand. One person regards one day above another, another regards every day alike. Each person must be fully convinced in his own mind. He who observes the day, observes it for the Lord, and he who eats, does so for the Lord, for he gives thanks to God; and he who eats not, for the Lord he does not eat, and gives thanks to God" (Romans 14:5-6).

Some believe these verses teach that those who live by the dietary laws of Torah are "weak" in their faith, and that the "strong" ones are those who pay no attention to such laws, believing they were annulled by the New Testament. They then apply this same errant rule to the feast days.

The above verses have to do with how we are to relate to those who are in a different place in their walk of faith. For instance, Paul says, "One person regards one day above another, another regards every day alike. Each person must be fully convinced in his own mind." The point being that we cannot *legislate* observance of the feasts. We must *not* try to force others into believing *what* we believe, *when* we believe it, for the Father instead wants each of His children to become convinced in their own minds.

In their book, *Take Hold*, Ariel and D'vorah Berkowitz explain: "Romans 14 and 15 describes the right behavior in handling an individual who has strong convictions over a disputable matter."

The Berkowitz's define "weak" as "delicate," and say use of the word refers to treating a person "delicately" when they "have strong convictions on a matter on which the Scriptures are not clear and therefore where there is likely to be difference of opinion among other believers."

They suggest being "gracious to such a one. If his strong conviction is not causing a serious problem in the body, give that person space and allow God to move in his life as needed over time (verses 3-4)." And, "According to verses 5-6 believers have room for their own personal convictions that are important to [them]..." [54]

This dispute may be over fasting versus not fasting. However, we conclude that, even though eating and how one regards a day are mentioned in the verses, the point being made is about *not passing judgments on people in disputable matters*.

On the other hand, these verses cannot be taken to mean that all days are equal in the sight of the Almighty, or that it is not important whether or not we honor His seventh-day Sabbath or His feast days. We are to observe these days, because—because it is to our benefit to do so.

Romans 14 is not suggesting that people celebrate the Sabbath any time they want, nor is it encouraging replacement holidays for the Father's appointed times.

Again, the issue is our *attitude* toward those who are in a different place in their faith walk.

In Romans 14:1 we are told to "accept the one who is weak in faith, but not for the purpose of passing judgment on his opinions." Stern says some have "strong trust" and some have "weak trust." We find both types among Jewish and non-Jewish Believers. Paul is *not* speaking of "weak Jewish faith" as some suggest. He is simply talking about weak Believers in general, and he is instructing those who are strong to help the weak grow in their faith.

---

54 Ariel & D'vorah Berkowitz, *Take Hold.* Chicago: First Fruits of Zion, 1999, p 218.

Batya Ruth Wootten

Batya and her husband, Angus, were early pioneers in the Messianic movement. Decades ago they began publishing the first Messianic Materials Catalogue, created to serve a fledgling new interest in Israel, the Jewish people, and relationships between Christians and Jews.

Batya read countless books about these subjects so she could write informed descriptions of them for the catalogue, and so discovered the great diversity of opinions about Israel's role in the world and about Israel's identity.

Hungering to truly understand "Israel," she began to cry out in desperation to her Heavenly Father, asking Him to show her *His* truth. As promised, He answered: "Call to Me and I will answer you, and I will tell you great and mighty things, which you do not know" (Jeremiah 33:3).

He began to open up the Scriptures to her, which led to her first book, *In Search of Israel,* and then to *The Olive Tree of Israel.* Next she wrote the comprehensive book, *Who Is Israel?* and its companion *Study Guide.* Then came *Ephraim and Judah: Israel Revealed.*

Batya's books represent decades of study, discussion, and prayer on this crucial issue. Readers have been transformed as they read about Israel in all its fullness. Lives continue to be changed as they see the truth about both the houses of Israel—Judah and Ephraim. It is a truth that is helping to restore a brotherhood broken apart long ago.

Batya's emphasis on the need for mercy and grace to both houses is helping to heal the wounds that began when Israel's Kingdom was divided into the Northern Kingdom of Israel and the Southern Kingdom of Judah.

Her newest book, *Israel's Feasts and Their Fullness,* represents many years of meticulous research, study, and prayerful writing. Several people have said of it: "This is the best book about the feasts that I have ever read."

We hope you will agree.

Batya is married to her best friend, Col. Angus Wootten (Ret.), author of the visionary book, *Restoring Israel's Kingdom,* plus a guide to the Torah commandments, *Take Two Tablets Daily.* Together they have ten children who have blessed them with many grandchildren and great-grandchildren.

Working as a team, Angus and Batya moved forward from the early days of the *House of David Catalogue* and began publishing the enlightening monthly Newsletter, the *House of David Herald,* which ultimately became a magazine, *The Messianic Israel Herald.*

They also developed the informative Messianic Israel web site: *www.mim.net* and *messianicisrael.com,* which in turn led to the founding of the *Messianic Israel Alliance—* a rapidly growing alliance of congregations, synagogues, and home fellowships that agree with *The Hope of Messianic Israel,* the statement of faith of the Messianic Israel Alliance. This cutting-edge Alliance is served by a dedicated Shepherds Council.

Together Angus and Batya continue to publish books that will serve the growing army of Messianic Israel, as well as raising up new leaders and drawing out their giftings. For this assignment they have been uniquely prepared by the God of Abraham, Isaac, and Jacob.

We know you will be blessed as you read their writings.

"Let the one who is taught share all good things with him who teaches" (Galatians 6:6).
If through this book a good thing has been accomplished in your life, please write and share your good news with me.

Batya Wootten
PO Box 700217, Saint Cloud, FL 34770
e-mail: batya@mim.net

The Hope of Messianic Israel

Messianic Israel believes Yeshua Ha'Natsree (Jesus of Nazareth) was and is the true Messiah, the Lion of Judah, the Branch Who will fully reunite all Israel; that He died and rose from the dead and lives at the right hand of the Almighty; and according to the ancient Holy Scriptures, Yeshua is YHVH Elohim appearing in the flesh, as Yeshua demonstrated in Himself (Deu 18:18-19; John 8:58; 10:33; Mat 12:6-8; 9:35; 15:31; Isa 11; 53; Micah 5:2-4; Luke 24:46; Isa 8:14; John 2:22; Acts 3:15-17; Heb 13:20; 1 John 4:2; 2 John 1:7; Rev 5:5; John 1:1).

Messianic Israel believes we are made righteous in Messiah Yeshua. (He is the heart of Abraham's un-conditional covenant.) The sign of the New Covenant is circumcision of the heart, which leads to confession, salvation, faith, grace, and to good works in Messiah. The conditional Mosaic covenant presents the eternal truths of Torah (YHVH's teaching and instructions) to His people, the hearing of which brings about blessing or curse (respond and be blessed, disobey and lack). In the New Covenant, Yeshua's Law is to be written on our hearts by the Spirit (Rom 4:13-16; 5:2; 10:10; 1 Pet 1:19; 2 Cor 5:21; Gal 3:16,29; Titus 3:5; Heb 10:38; 1 John 1:9; Eph 2:8; James 2:14; Deu 28; Ezek 36:26; Jer 31:31-33; Heb 10:16; Gal 2:16; John 5:46; 10;30; 14:2; 15:10).

Messianic Israel is a people whose heart's desire is to fully reunite the olive tree of Israel—both branches —Ephraim and Judah—into one, redeemed, nation of Israel—through Messiah Yeshua. They seek to arouse Ephraim from obscurity, and by example, to awaken Judah to the Messiah—and thus to hasten both Yeshua's return to Earth and the restoration of the promised Kingdom to Israel (Mat 6:10; 12:25; 21:43; 24:43; Luke 22:29-30; Mark 13:34; Luke 22:29-30; 2 Chr 11:4; Eze 37:15-28; Jer 11:10,16; 2:18,21; Rom 11:17,24; Eph 2:11-22; Acts 1:6).

Messianic Israel deems the Jewish people to be the identifiable representatives and offspring of Judah and "the children of Israel, his companions," and that non-Jewish followers of the Messiah from all nations have been, up to now, the unidentifiable represen-tatives and offspring of Ephraim and "all the house of Israel, his companions" (Gen 48:19; Hosea 1-2; 5:3; Eze 37:16; Jer 31:6-9; Gen 15:2-5; 26:3; 28:4; Heb 11:9; Isa 56:3,6-8; Eph 2:11-22).

Messianic Israel affirms that the Jewish people have been kept identifiable as seed of the patriarch Jacob, YHVH's covenant people, to preserve His Holy Torah (Law), Feasts, and Shabbat (Sabbath); that the salvation of the Jewish people through their acceptance of Messiah

Yeshua, will be the crowning act of mankind's redemption, and is necessary for the restoration of the Kingdom to Israel. Further, the Father plans that Ephraim, they being the "wild olive branch," stimulate Judah to want what they have; they are called to walk in a way that will make Judah jealous of their relationship with the God of Israel (Gen 48:19; Isa 11:13; 37:31,32; Zec 2:12; Eze 37:15-28; Hosea 1:7; Rom 10:19; 11:11,14; Mat 23:39).

Messianic Israel believes the non-Jewish followers of Yeshua are predominantly returning Ephraim, those who were once among the Gentiles/Goyim/Nations as "LoAmi,"or "Not a people," but have now been restored to the commonwealth of Israel through their covenant with Israel's Messiah; that, they are no more Gentiles/ Goyim/of the Nations, but fulfill the promised restoration of uprooted Ephraim, and Jacob's prophecy that Ephraim would become "melo hagoyim," the "full-ness of the Gentiles/Goyim/ Nations." As Ephraim, they have been kept in mystery until recently, being used to preserve the testimony of Yeshua, the Messiah of all Israel. Their awakening, recognition, and performance as Ephraim, and their union with Judah, is a necessity for salvation of "all" Israel, and the restoration of the Kingdom to Israel (Gen 48:19; Hosea 1:9-10; 5:3; 8:8; Amos 9:9; Jer 31:18-19; Zec 10:7; Rom 9:24-26; 11:26; Eph 2:11-22).

Messianic Israel declares that Believers in Yeshua were not meant to replace Judah as Israel, but as "Ephraim," they are part of the called out ones (ekklesia), and in these latter-days, the Father is leading them to, whenever scripturally possible, join with Judah; that Judah (faithful Jewish ones who will receive Messiah) and Ephraim (faithful non-Jewish Messiah followers) ultimately will fulfill the destiny of the two houses of Israel: that together they might fulfill the prophesies about the one, unified, victorious people of Israel (Jer 31:9; Rom 8:29; Col 1:15,18; 2:12; Heb 12:22-24; Lev 23:2-36; Exo 19:5; 1 Pet 1:1; 2:9; Jer 3:18; 23:6; Zec 8:13; 12:1-5; Mat 25:31-46; Exo 12:48-49; Num 15:15-16; Isa 56:3,6-8).

Messianic Israel maintains that up to this general time "blindness in part" has happened to all (both houses) of Israel, and as the blinders are lifted, non-Jewish followers in Yeshua will gain insight into their role as Ephraim and become defenders of scriptural Torah and of Judah, and due to this character change, many Jewish people will accept Yeshua as Messiah. This process has begun as indicated through the Messianic Jewish movement (Judah), the Christian Zionism movement (Ephraim), and the Messianic Israel movement (union of Judah and Ephraim) (Isa 8:14; 11:13; Rom 11:25,26; Jer 33:14-16; 31:18-19; Ezek 37:15-28).

The reunion and full restoration of the two houses:

This is the hope that burns in the hearts of those of Messianic Israel...

Who Is Israel?
Enlarged Edition
by Batya Wootten

This phenomenal book is causing an awakening in the Body of Messiah because it clearly explains the truth about "both the houses of Israel," (Isaiah 8:14). It explains who is indeed an Israelite. This awareness has caused a reformation in the Body of Messiah. Read this solution-driven book and see the truth that is inspiring Believers everywhere!

Who is Israel? Why do *you* need to know? Knowing who you are and where you are going is vital to your relationship with the God of Israel.

Reading this book will inspire and encourage you, even change your life. It will help you discover your own Hebraic Heritage and put your feet on the road to Zion. It will enable you to: Understand Israel, the Church, the Bible — The mystery of the "fullness of the Gentiles" — The "blindness of Israel" — The Father's master plan for Israel. It will answer: Why you feel something is missing in your life — Why you have a love for Israel and Jewish people — And why you feel an urge to celebrate the feasts of Israel.

This handbook will move you from religion to relationship. The Biblical truths unveiled in this volume will help: Put an end to "Christian" anti-Semitism and heal divisions in the Body of Messiah, as well as lead us back to our first love: Messiah Yeshua.

This enlightening book includes the following chapters: Believing What Abraham Believed — Israel: A Blessing — Jacob's Firstborn Heir — Ephraim: A Profile — Yankees and Rebels — LoAmmi: Not A People — Many Israels, One Israel — A Priceless Gift — Chosen To Choose — The Blood, The Redeemer, And Physical Israel — Literal or Spiritual? — Israel: A Mystery Until — "Holey" Doctrines — More Tattered Theories — Is Judah All Israel? — Leaving Elementary Things Behind — From Orphans To Heirs — The Olive Tree of Israel — One Law, One People — The Two

Passover in all its Fullness

Witnesses And Their Fullness — Called to Be Watchmen — Return, O Virgin Israel! — Yeshua: Epitome of All That Is Israel — An Israel Yet To Come. This Enlarged Edition includes Maps and Charts and an Addendum about current Jewish genetic research.
ISBN 1-886987-03-3   Paper, 304 pages $14.95.

Also Available in Spanish!

¿Quién es Israel?

Por Batya Wootten

Traducido al Español por Natalie Pavlik
ISBN 1-886987-08-4 $14.95

Who Is Israel?
A Study Guide

This *Study Guide* is an excellent companion volume to *Who Is Israel?* It can be used as a 12 or 24 week Study Course. The study plan is simple and does not require a great deal of preparation by the leaders. The goal is to help people come to an understanding of Israel and their part in Israel.

The *Study Guide* contains the printed Scripture verses that correspond to each lesson in *Who Is Israel?* These can be read and discussed by the group. Sample questions are listed in the *Study Guide*, with answers in the back. Reading and discussing the selected texts among brethren builds up your faith and makes Scripture come alive with new meaning.

If you want fellowship with Believers of like mind, order a case of these *Study Guides* and get started today!

ISBN 1-886987-08-4   Paper, 288 pages, $12.95
Case of Ten: $85.00 (plus shipping)

Israel's Feasts and their Fullness
by Batya Wootten

Growing interest in the feasts of Israel has resulted in some confusion and misunderstanding about how Believers in Messiah Yeshua are to celebrate the feasts.

Fortunately, the Father has raised up a voice of clarity in the midst of muddied waters. In her indomitable and delightful style, Batya Wootten has written a clear, concise, informative, well researched, yet entertaining and highly enjoyable book about the feasts of Israel. At last we are told how we can celebrate with the joy and freedom of Messiah Yeshua, yet with reverence for the accuracy of the Holy Scriptures and due respect for the honorable truths of Judaism.

Here you will find trustworthy information on how to celebrate each of the feasts. Included are "Celebration Instruction Guides" for the Sabbath, Havdalah, and Passover. Additionally, there are numerous charts, graphs, tables, and exciting graphics.

Batya continues in the style that has endeared her to so many of her readers. She has written of the need for grace and mercy to both the houses of Israel—Judah and Ephraim. She encourages us to begin to dance and sing and celebrate the presence of the Almighty in our midst!

Get ready for a delightful ride into the Kingdom of God's feasts. This is a book you can't put down and one that you will to refer to for years to come.

ISBN 1-886987-02-5   Paper 384 pages $17.95

Color Printed Celebration Instruction Guides

$2.00 each (includes shipping).
Please specify:
1. Shabbat Guide
2. Havdalah Guide
3. Passover Guide
4. Messianic Jewish Passover Guide